W9-CDU-777

A12900 280080

WITHDRAWN

ILLINOIS CENTRAL COLLEGE
PN3448.P8A8
STACKS
The modern confessional novel.

PN
3448   AXTHELM
.P8   The mode   A12900 280080
A8   novel

Illinois Central College
Learning Resource Center

THE MODERN CONFESSIONAL NOVEL

The

Modern

Confessional

Novel

BY PETER M. AXTHELM

ILLINOIS CENTRAL COLLEGE
LEARNING RESOURCE CENTER

NEW HAVEN AND LONDON, YALE UNIVERSITY PRESS, 1967

30473

PN
3448
.P8
A8

Copyright © 1967 by Yale University.
Designed by Anne Rajotte,
set in Times Roman type,
and printed in the United States of America by
The Carl Purington Rollins Printing-Office of the
Yale University Press, New Haven, Connecticut.
Distributed in Canada by McGill University Press.
All rights reserved. This book may not be
reproduced, in whole or in part, in any form
(except by reviewers for the public press),
without written permission from the publishers.
Library of Congress catalog card number: 67–13428

Yale College Series

The tradition of undergraduate writing and publishing has long been a very lively one at Yale, as witnessed by the large number of periodicals, journalistic or literary in character, which have appeared on the Yale campus. These, however, fail to give an accurate picture of the high proportion of good and original scholarly writing which is also done by undergraduates. The excellence of many of the Honors theses written by Yale Seniors made it desirable some years ago to give the most deserving of them the circulation which publication in printed form could provide. Between 1941 and 1957 ten volumes were published in the Undergraduate Prize Essays Series and two in the Scholars of the House Series. The authors of several of these essays have gone on to fulfill amply the promise of their early scholarly efforts. More recently the growing number of theses of outstanding merit has encouraged Yale College and the Yale University Press to establish this new YALE COLLEGE SERIES with the hope that every year it will be possible to publish some of the best work by the Honors majors in the Senior Class. The selection, which is necessarily a very rigorous one, was performed for the Class of 1965 by a faculty committee made up of Messrs. S. W. Reed, M. I. J. Griffin, and E. M. Waith, Chairman.

Georges May
Dean of Yale College

ACKNOWLEDGMENTS

I am indebted to Roger Salomon, a patient and perceptive adviser, who worked with me on this book in the Yale College Intensive Program in English. Mr. Salomon's suggestions and criticisms helped to decide the scope and form of the study, and his sincere interest made the entire project a pleasure. I should also thank Professors Martin Price and Robert Penn Warren, who helped me develop a sound critical perspective on modern novels, and especially Davis P. Harding, who contributed both sound judgment and an unflagging wit during the arduous weeks before the book was completed.

I am grateful to the publishers who granted permission to use quotations from the important confessional novels:

Saul Bellow, *Herzog,* copyright © 1961, 1963, 1964, by permission of the Viking Press, Inc., and Weidenfeld & Nicolson Ltd.

Albert Camus, *The Fall,* trans. Justin O'Brien, copyright © 1956, by permission of Random House and Secker, Martin and Warburg Ltd.

André Gide, *The Immoralist,* trans. Dorothy Bussy, copyright © 1930, 1958, by permission of Random House and Hamish-Hamilton Ltd.

William Golding, *Free Fall,* copyright © 1962, by permission of Harcourt, Brace & World, Inc., and Faber & Faber Ltd.

Acknowledgments

Arthur Koestler, *Darkness at Noon,* copyright © 1961, by permission of the Macmillan Company and A. D. Peters.

Jean-Paul Sartre, *Nausea,* trans. Lloyd Alexander, copyright © 1965, by permission of New Directions Publishing Corporation and Lloyd Alexander.

New York   Peter M. Axthelm
November 1966

TABLE OF CONTENTS

In the end one experiences only oneself.
Nietzsche, *Thus Spoke Zarathustra*

Introduction

In 1948, Thomas Merton, a Trappist monk, published his autobiography, *The Seven Storey Mountain*. The work, which has been called "a twentieth century form of the *Confessions* of St. Augustine," begins with a bleak image of disintegration:

> On the last day of January 1915, under the sign of the Water Bearer, in the year of a great war . . . I came into the world. Free by nature, in the image of God, I was nevertheless the prisoner of my own violence and my own selfishness, in the image of the world into which I was born. That world was a

picture of Hell, full of men like myself . . . living in fear and
hopeless self-contradictory hungers.

Not many hundreds of miles away from the house in which
I was born, they were picking up the men who rotted in the
rainy ditches among the dead horses.[1]

With its tortured and paradoxical freedom, its evocation of hell,
and its recognition of the contradictions and drives within man,
this vision is remarkably similar to the characteristic world-view
of the modern confessional hero. It is separated from that view,
however, by the presence of the "image of God," which points
toward Merton's religious solution to the vast problem of modern
existence. After twenty-six years in such a world, he retreats into
the most rigorous of monasteries, which he calls a "school in
which we learn from God how to be happy."

The beginning of Merton's religious autobiography reveals a
deeply personal awareness of evil; this same awareness is the
starting point for Augustine's *Confessions,* as well as for the self-
examination which the modern hero undertakes. The Trappist
monk, however, is the most uncharacteristic of modern men, a
man capable of moving *outside* the limitations of existence into
an isolated spiritual world. What of the man who cannot find an
"image of God" amid the chaos which surrounds him? What of
the man who cannot look forward to some future life, and so
must confront his present existence in all its dark and terrifying
forms? This is the crucial question for our time, the challenge
which the modern confessional novel attempts to answer.

The seeds of this challenge lie at the origins of confessional
literature, in the work of Augustine. The author of the *Confessions*
shows an acute sensitivity to the problems and conflicts of man's
inner self, as well as a broad consciousness of evil. Because of his
intense concern with the self, Augustine is often cited as a pre-
cursor of existentialism. In his brilliant and unflinching percep-

1. Thomas Merton, *The Seven Storey Mountain* (New York, Signet,
1962), p. 9.

2

tions, he approaches many of the paradoxes and problems which continue to dominate man's struggle with his existence. When he reaches the climactic moment of confrontation with such an existential dilemma, however, Augustine is forced to resolve it by using Christian metaphysics. It is this transition from internal to external methods which introduces the crucial dichotomy in the confessional tradition. Some fifteen centuries later, this dichotomy produces the modern challenge to confession.

One of the paradoxes which Augustine confronts is expressed in his cry to God about his sins as a young man:

> Bodily desire, like a morass, and adolescent sex welling up within me exuded mists which clouded over and obscured my heart, so that I could not distinguish the clear light of true love from the murk of lust . . . I was tossed and spilled, floundering in the broiling sea of my fornication, and you said no word.[2]

The striking final phrase of this passage is emphasized. "You did not restrain me," he repeats; "You were silent then, and I went on my way, farther and farther." The question implied in this phrase is not theological, but existential; it is the question of a man desperately seeking self-understanding without the aid of revelation. When man dares to wonder how an all-good Deity can allow him to fall victim to turbulent and uncontrollable passions, serene faith gives way to confusion and anguish.

In this passage, Augustine approaches the tone of Job, torn between faith and bewilderment, love of God and outrage at injustice. "I will not refrain my mouth," Job cries. "I will speak in the anguish of my spirit; I will complain in the bitterness of my soul."[3] But Augustine retreats from this crisis into a religious solution which leaves the existential question virtually un-

2. St. Augustine, *Confessions,* trans. R. S. Pine-Coffin (London, Penguin, 1961), p. 43.
3. *Job* 7:11. (All biblical citations are from the King James Version.)

answered. "I might have listened more attentively to your voice from the clouds," he says, referring to the "voice" of scriptural texts on sex and adultery. In the voice of Scripture, as in the Voice from the Whirlwind which speaks to Job, the passions and sufferings of man are fitted into a pattern of justice, yet neither of these voices can fully convince us that the problem presented by the hero has been resolved. The sense of tension and frustration—of the unanswered question—remains. As Richard Sewall points out in regard to the conclusion of the *Book of Job,* "The universe seems secure only to those who do not question too far."[4]

Augustine, however, insists on pursuing the problems of existence. His pursuit leads him to the question of freedom:

> We learn better in a free spirit of curiosity than under fear and compulsion. But your law, O God, permits the free flow of curiosity to be stemmed by force. From the schoolmaster's cane to the ordeal of martydom, your law prescribes bitter medicine to retrieve us from the noxious pleasures which cause us to desert you.[5]

This is a lucid portrayal of the problem which comes to the center of modern consciousness in Ivan Karamazov's "Legend of the Grand Inquisitor." But Augustine's attempt to reconcile "free spirit" with "God's force" produces only an unconvincing gesture of rationalization: "It is true that these [earlier] studies taught me many useful words, but the same words can be learnt by studying something that matters, and that is the safe course for a boy to follow."

Throughout the *Confessions,* Augustine continues to ask the enduring existential questions; but as a Christian theologian committed to the justification of God's cosmos, he cannot answer them in the same terms. This self-imposed limitation does not

4. Richard B. Sewall, *The Vision of Tragedy* (New Haven, Yale University Press, 1959), p. 24.
5. St. Augustine, p. 35.

obscure his tremendous human insight, but it does produce the sharply defined dichotomy which William Barrett describes:

> The duality that gave rise on the one hand to Augustine the existential lyricist of religious experience and on the other to Augustine the formal theologian (thinking with the concepts of Greek metaphysics) is one that lay concealed beneath all the centuries of medieval philosophy that followed; but it did not erupt into painful consciousness until the modern period, when the containing structure of the church, which had held the conflicting elements together in a kind of suspension, could no longer serve this purpose.[6]

The moment of "painful consciousness" arrives in the second half of the nineteenth century, when Dostoevsky takes his hero underground, where the light of revelation cannot enter, and forces him to seek his primary causes in the depths of his own being. Ivan Karamazov rejects the enslavement of the free spirit and the Underground Man lashes out at rationalism and optimism. The metaphysical side of Augustine's vision, which has been carried on through Hegel, "is at the end of the line . . . once the spirit of existential revolt enters the world."[7] Man is left to find the meaning of life within himself; this, in turn, demands a new mode of self-examination.

Traditional Christianity sees self-knowledge as an approach to God; St. Bernard describes this process in his *Meditations:* "I will returne from outward things to inward, and from the inward I will ascend to the Superiour. . . . For by how much I profit, and goe forward in the knowledge of my selfe, by so much the neerer I approach to the knowledge of God."[8] When Nietzsche denies

6. William Barrett, *Irrational Man* (Garden City, N.Y., Doubleday Anchor, 1962), p. 96.
7. Ibid., p. 97.
8. St. Bernard of Clairvaux, *St. Bernard His Meditations,* trans. "W.P." (London, 1631–32); cited in Louis Martz, *The Poetry of Meditation* (New Haven, Yale University Press, 1954), pp. 118–19.

the existence of the goal of this kind of confession, he simultaneously suggests a new direction for the process of self-scrutiny in the modern world: "God is dead, says Nietzsche, and European man if he were more honest, courageous, and had keener eyes for what went on in the depths of his own soul would know that this death has taken place there."[9] This is the challenge to modern man. He must explore his own being, not in an effort to move closer to God, but in a quest for a meaning which does not depend on God or on any force outside the self. One response to this challenge is the modern confessional novel. No attempt need be made here to detail the development of the confessional tradition during the centuries between St. Augustine and the modern existentialists. It is worthwhile, however, to mention certain trends which may illuminate the modern confessional genre.

The Reformation, by questioning the theological "rules" for confession, produced a form which placed more emphasis on individual thought. Franklin Baumer points this out:

> "Christian," in John Bunyan's *Pilgrim's Progress,* pursuing his lonely way, without help of priests or sacraments, toward the Celestial City was a typical Protestant. Likewise the Puritan diarist who in the secret of his closet recorded his daily struggle with sin. . . . The Puritan had to work out his own rules and assume responsibility for them.[10]

As the diarists moved further away from the rigidly schematized meditations of the medieval monks, their journals began to play a significant role, as Kenneth Murdock indicates, in "the evolution in the seventeenth century from the older stereotyped and 'formal' life to something closer to . . . complete portraiture of the individual."[11]

9. Barrett, p. 13.

10. Franklin L. V. Baumer, *Main Currents of Western Thought* (New York, Alfred A. Knopf, 1962), p. 170.

11. Kenneth B. Murdock, *Literature and Theology in Colonial New England* (Cambridge, Harvard University Press, 1949), p. 134.

As journals became popular and more diarists began to write with the intention of publication, the confessional form was eventually employed in nonreligious works. Rousseau's *Confessions* (1781–88) were followed in the nineteenth century by numerous confessions by the Romantics, such as Musset and Chateaubriand in France and de Quincey in England. It was only in Russia, however, where such writers as Gogol, Lermontov, and Turgenev experimented with first-person narration and various new techniques, that confessional writings began to focus on the problems which would be of primary concern to Dostoevsky and his successors.

Nikolai Gogol is probably the most important forerunner of Dostoevsky among modern writers. He was among the first to recognize the fictional possibilities of the "ordinary" man, the petty official or clerk whose personal pains are compounded by an overwhelming sense of anonymity and humiliation; it is from this class that Dostoevsky's Underground Man emerges. The hero of Gogol's "Memoirs of a Madman" (1935) attempts to counter his humiliating situation with exotic romantic dreams, foreshadowing the conflicts within the Underground Man. Lermontov's *A Hero of Our Time* (1940), which Mirsky called "the greatest Russian prose ever written, if we judge by the standards of perfection and not by those of wealth,"[12] was a great advance for the novel form in Russia. The preface, written a year later, emphasizes the separation of the author from the hero—a distinction which is important for all first-person narration and particularly for the confessional novel. In *The Diary of a Superfluous Man* (1850), Turgenev explores the theme of humiliation which becomes central to the Dostoevskian hero; more important, he signals the decline of the romantic hero—an ineffective idealist who was becoming increasingly superfluous to modern life.

12. D. S. Mirsky, *A History of Russian Literature from Its Beginnings to 1900*, ed. Francis J. Whitfield (New York, Vintage, 1958), p. 163.

Frederick Hoffman describes the superfluous man in more detail:

> The very nature of his romantic despair, disillusion or melancholy is shown to come from an "unproductive" or an "unrealistic," in any case an "unprofitable" set of circumstances. He does no one any good and the scope of his emotional extravagances is judged as tedious and perhaps a bit ridiculous.[13]

Some aspects of *Notes from the Underground* are clearly derived from the ideas of Gogol and other Russian authors. As a whole, however, the work is strikingly original. Its origins can be seen in reaction to rather than in derivation from eighteenth- and nineteenth-century confessions; it constitutes a biting attack on the optimistic memoirs of Rousseau and the entire rationalist creed that man acts for his own best interests. The only previous confessional work which shows a positive similarity to the *Notes* —in its mode of self-examination although not in its ultimate world-view—is that of St. Augustine.

The dominant characteristics of the modern confessional novel will be explained in the subsequent treatments of individual authors. At this point, we will offer a basic definition of this type of novel, to provide a framework for more detailed considerations and to indicate the scope of the genre. The confessional novel presents a hero, at some point in his life, examining his past as well as his innermost thoughts, in an effort to achieve some form of perception. A closer consideration of these four elements will clarify this definition.

The confessional hero often introduces himself to the reader at the outset; taken together, these introductions provide a vivid image of this type of hero. "I am a sick man," declares the Underground Man. "I am a spiteful man. I am an unattractive man."

13. Frederick J. Hoffman, *Samuel Beckett: The Language of Self* (New York, Dutton, 1962), p. 10.

In Sartre's *Nausea,* the hero's journal begins: "Something has happened to me, I can't doubt it any more. It came as an illness does." The narrator of Golding's *Free Fall* describes himself as "a burning amateur, torn by the irrational and incoherent, searching and self-condemned." In the opening line of *Herzog,* Bellow's hero wonders if he is out of his mind. Koestler's *Darkness at Noon* begins with the slamming of a door and the hero's reflection, "A fine generation we have produced."

This, then, is the confessional hero—afflicted and unbalanced, disillusioned and groping for meaning. He faces many of the same problems which confront every modern hero but is distinguished by his reaction to them. He views his condition not with anger but with a deep internal pain; he rejects external rebellion in favor of self-laceration. His suffering originates not in the chaos of the world but in the chaos within the self, and for him the only possible order or value must be found in self-understanding. After *Notes from the Underground,* this hero becomes increasingly intellectual, capable of philosophical meditations and prone to literary allusions. However, he never loses his huge capacity for suffering and is constantly torn by violent emotions and uncontrollable compulsions.

The hero's confession often takes place in a cell, an underground hole, or a dark city; at other times, he tells his story to another character in a setting reminiscent of the religious confession. Whatever the external forces upon him, he ultimately looks inward, suspending the course of external events while he probes his past and considers his existence.

When Montaigne wrote his "personal essays" in the sixteenth century, he justified the idea of writing about himself: "Authors communicate themselves to the world by some special and extrinsic mark: I am the first to do so by my general being, as Michel de Montaigne, not as a grammarian or a poet or a lawyer."[14] In

14. Erich Auerbach, *Mimesis: The Representation of Reality in Western Literature* (Garden City, N.Y., Doubleday Anchor, 1957), p. 251.

portraying his "general being," Montaigne does not hesitate to flaunt logical and literary conventions; he skips over certain steps of reasoning and repeats and embellishes incidents which especially interest him. Erich Auerbach points out that this fluctuation of intensity is central to the purpose of the work:

> Montaigne's apparently fanciful method, which obeys no preconceived plan but adapts itself elastically to the changes of his own being, is basically a strictly experimental method, the only method which conforms to such a subject.[15]

The confessional hero, driven by compulsions he scarcely understands and exploring unknown depths of the soul, must approach his self-examination with a similarly experimental method. His confession may assume the relatively orderly form of the journal, or it may be a hesitant, halting process, accelerated by external interrogators. Temporal order ceases to define the course of his confession, as time is manipulated or suspended while the hero considers events from various periods in his past.

Golding's hero, Sammy Mountjoy, describes time as "a memory, a sense of shuffle fold and coil, of that day nearer than this because more important." This concept leads to an important defining quality of the confessional mode—the principle of selection. It is this principle which offers the distinction between the confessional novel and the stream-of-consciousness fiction of writers like Joyce and Faulkner. The internal monologue gives the reader an impression of random thought, of a mind being assailed by a series of ideas over which it exercises no power of selection. Actually, the impression of a hero without the power of selection can be achieved only through a very rigorous selective process on the part of the author; Leon Edel explains the early critical misunderstanding of *Ulysses:*

> Critics failed to understand that Joyce was exercising close selection and arrangement even when he seemed to dredge

15. Ibid., p. 255.

10

up a great deal of unrelated associational material. His selection was addressed to the creating of an illusion *that there had been no illusion.*[16]

In the confessional novel, there is no such effort to project an illusion of random flow. The hero confronts certain events because they are most important to him, others because they are forced into his mind by external forces, and still others because of compulsions which he himself cannot fully understand. The selective process is that of the hero, not of the author.

The characteristic techniques which have been developed within the confessional genre will be discussed later. Perhaps the two most important are the double and the use of irony by both the author and the hero. The double—a more psychologically complex version of the mirror symbol—is used consistently to express the confessional hero's relations with others in terms of self-discovery. Irony is one of the primary controlling factors in the confessional novel; it maintains the author's detachment from his hero and also gives the hero a weapon with which to destroy any romantic notions which might lure him away from the central purpose of his confession.

The final aspect of our basic definition is the search for perception. This goal is inherited from the religious idea of purgation or absolution through confession. The vision sought by the modern hero, however, is unrelated to the forgiveness of any external religion. It can best be described as self-understanding or perception rather than purgation. "I am writing for myself alone," he asserts, as he probes deeper into his soul. He uncovers elements of pain, humiliation, and guilt, yet continues his quest as his suffering increases, hoping at last to find some perception of the truth that lies at the center of his existence. Only in this can he complete what the Underground Man calls his "corrective punishment."

16. Leon Edel, *The Modern Psychological Novel* (New York, Universal Library, 1964), p. 22.

Introduction

To begin a fuller examination of the most important themes and characteristics of the modern confessional genre, we must turn to the master of the confession in modern times. Dostoevsky's treatment of confession is so original and so varied that he introduces many of the concepts which remain central to the problem of self-examination in the novel.

1. ORIGINS OF THE MODERN CONFESSIONAL NOVEL:

Dostoevsky

In *Notes from the Underground,* Fyodor Dostoevsky provides a prescription for the genre of the modern confessional novel. He employs the confessional form of the French Romantics and his Russian predecessors like Gogol, Lermontov, and Turgenev, but he intensifies it and turns it inward; his central character is concerned not with exposition but with self-discovery and what he terms "corrective punishment." "Where are the primary causes on which I am to build?" the Underground Man asks. "Where are my foundations?"[1] His answers can be found only through a sincere and single-purposed self-analysis.

1. Fyodor Dostoevsky, *Notes from the Underground,* trans. Constance Garnett, included in *Three Short Novels of Dostoevsky* (Garden City, N.Y., Doubleday Anchor, 1960), p. 193. (Henceforth quotations from this novel will be identified by page numbers in parentheses.)

13

The pivotal role of this novel in Dostoevsky's development and in the confessional tradition is reflected in its two-part structure. Part I presents the remarkable anti-hero and his dark, tormented view of the world. His brilliantly sustained monologue contains many of the author's most important ideas—ideas which are more fully developed in the great novels that follow. But although this section looks forward to Dostoevsky's later work, its form unites it to the past. The hero's thoughts are directed outward; he even refers petulantly to his audience, saying, "If you won't deign to give me your attention, I will drop your acquaintance" (p. 211). This self-conscious concern with the impression he is making prevents him from embarking on a real self-analysis; his words remain linked to the expositional technique of earlier confessions.

In Part II, on the other hand, the Underground Man justifies his claim that "I write only for myself." His tortured philosophizing and mental exercises give way to direct confrontations with certain crucial events in his life. Abandoning his efforts to defend his actions, he faces them directly in a series of vividly recalled episodes. The result is the first confessional novel.

One of the central aspects of *Notes from the Underground,* and one which deviates sharply from the romantic confessions preceding it, is the preoccupation with suffering. Consciousness itself is a form of suffering for Dostoevsky's anti-hero, who asks, "Can a man of perception respect himself at all?" For him, the confession, by providing more knowledge, can only increase his suffering. Yet he is compelled to go on with it, partly because of the sort of perverse joy he finds in suffering and partly because he must seek answers to his pressing questions about who he is.

Early in his notes, the writer wonders if the whole world might not be caught up in a metaphysic of suffering. "Does not man, perhaps, love something besides well-being? Perhaps he is just as fond of suffering? Perhaps suffering is just as great a benefit to him as well-being?" (p. 209) When he turns to the events of his own past, it becomes clear that such a principle certainly governs his

14

actions. He is often faced with a choice in which he might withdraw from a painful situation, yet he unfailingly probes such
situations to their most degrading depths. As he goes to see his
school acquaintance Simonov, for example, he thinks:

> Climbing up to his fourth story, I was thinking that the man
> disliked me and that it was a mistake to go and see him.
> But as it always happened that such reflections impelled me,
> as though purposely, to put myself in a false position, I went
> in. (p. 232)

Thus the Underground Man plunges on through his life and
through his confession.

The anti-hero calls himself a "paradoxical fellow," and his
notes are built on a series of paradoxes and dichotomies. The
fundamental duality presents the hero's individual self against
the external world. Dostoevsky expressed his concern with this
problem in a letter to his brother in 1847, seventeen years before
he wrote this novel:

> Of course, terrible is the dissonance, terrible the imbalance
> which society creates in us. External and internal things
> should be in equilibrium. For, lacking external experiences,
> those of the inner life gain the upper hand, and that is most
> dangerous. The nerves and fantasy then take up too much
> room in one's consciousness. Every external happening,
> from want of habit, seems colossal and is somehow frighten-
> ing. We begin to fear life.[2]

The Underground Man is a victim of just such an imbalance; he is
reflecting the author's view when he says he is suffering from "a
real thorough-going illness."

This basic division of the hero from the world is set up in the
first section of *Notes from the Underground*. The writer affirms

2. Robert L. Jackson, *Dostoevsky's Underground Man in Russian Literature* (The Hague, Mouton and Co., 1958), p. 29.

his will and freedom and assails the wall of rationalism and determination. He revels in his denial of "laws and the fact that two and two make four" and claims that he will never be reconciled to them. Ultimately, however, he must admit "I have not the strength" to batter this wall. He can only withdraw, saying, "It is better to do nothing! Better conscious inertia! And so hurrah for the underground!" (p. 211) And in the underground, his paradoxical situation remains and expands.

Having established his individual will and then withdrawn it from the external world, the Underground Man faces another aspect of his paradoxical existence. He must live with his own "overacute consciousness," yet he is impotent to alleviate the pain he feels. When he tries to escape it in flights of romanticism or efforts to communicate with others, his consciousness drags him back to the suffering of his underground world. This paradox is at the center of his thoughts in Part II of the novel.

A striking example of the manner in which he dramatically jolts himself out of any romantic notion occurs in his recollection of visits to his friend Anton Antonych:

> I only went to see him when that phase came over me, when my dreams had reached such a point of bliss that it became essential at once to embrace my fellows and all mankind . . . I had to call on Anton Antonych, however, on Tuesday—his day at home; so I had always to time my passionate desire to embrace humanity so that it might fall on a Tuesday. (pp. 230–31)

Throughout the notes, he continues to fluctuate wildly between cynicism and romanticism, imagined heroism and self-debasement, and feelings of superiority and inferiority toward others. In these frenzied transitions, Dostoevsky creates a raw and vivid image of the "overacute consciousness."

It is significant that Part II of the novel begins with the sensuous image of "the wet snow." In this, the confessional section, such tangible images begin to replace the abstractions that comprised the first section. His attention turns to the real, external world and his relations with it. In fact, the entire process of self-discovery in the Underground Man's confession is achieved through an understanding of his relations with others.

His observations of other people begin in Part I, with his view of the office personnel with whom he worked when he was twenty-four. While his efforts to locate himself in (or out of) this milieu foreshadow the theme of Part II, they remain full of the paradoxical flux of the opening section of the novel. The Underground Man affirms his individuality amidst these men who show not "the slightest self-consciousness" about their faults; yet his own acute consciousness leads only to a terrible inferiority complex, so extreme that "I dropped my eyes almost every time I met anyone." He compounds the paradox in his recollection of those days, when he denies the very individuality he has suffered for, claiming a twisted kind of normalcy: "I was a coward and a slave. I say this without the slightest embarrassment. Every decent man of our age must be a coward and a slave. That is his normal condition" (p. 217).

The recollection of the office emphasizes the consciousness of the Underground Man; the following scene balances it with a concentration on his possibilities for action. The narrator's craving for action is so extreme that he would accept even the most painful act. When he sees a man hurled from a poolroom window, he admits, "I actually envied the gentleman." But even such a pitiful desire for action is frustrated; when he tries to pick a fight with an officer, he is simply ignored. "I could have forgiven blows," he says, "but I could not forgive his having moved me without noticing me."

The quality of being different, of being at least noticeable, is the one thing that sustains the hero, so he is compelled to seek revenge for this affront. He harbors his determination for years, and when he finally sees an opportunity to meet the officer during his walks on the Nevsky, he goes through a frantic and painful period of preparation for the collision. His triumph is comic:

> I closed my eyes, and we ran full tilt, shoulder to shoulder, against one another! I did not budge an inch and passed him on a perfectly equal footing! He did not even look around and pretended not to notice it; but he was only pretending, I am convinced of that. (p. 227)

Pitiful and self-deluding though it is, this is a kind of victory for the Underground Man. He has acted, however feebly, and maintained the one principle for existence in his underground world—individuality, or what he calls "my dignity."

The officer in this episode is the antithesis of the narrator. He is the man of action, insensitive and powerful, representative of the entire external world. The hero's closest contact with him can be only a brush of shoulders; more often, as on a previous attempt at a collision, the hero will only "fly to one side like a ball" as such a man approaches. But with the officer, the Underground Man can at least delude himself enough to maintain some pride; in his second meeting with an opposite—his clash with Zverkov—he can no longer do so, and probes to the deepest degradation of his situation.

The beginning of the affair with Zverkov reveals the tortured compulsion behind so many of the hero's acts. As he goes to see his friend Simonov, he knows he is not wanted; yet he not only intrudes on the group but also invites himself to the dinner they are planning. He sees their combination of indifference and distaste for his company, but he knows that he will not draw back until he has exacted the fullest measure of humiliation: "What made me furious was that I knew for certain that I should go, that I should make a point of going; and the more tactless, the more unseemly my going would be, the more certainly I would go" (p. 236). The dinner party itself is a treatment of the possibilities of heroism in the Underground Man. He snatches every feeble victory he can imagine, then is inevitably plunged back into reality. In the symbolic yellow stain on his only pants, he bears the ineradicable sign of his inferiority. With utmost anguish, he must bow before the supreme man of action, Zverkov.

Thinking about the affair before it happens, the hero reminisces about his school days, recalling a tainted victory over Zverkov similar to his clash with the officer on the Nevsky. In their flight, he says, "I got the better of him on that occasion, but, though Zverkov was stupid, he was lively and impudent, and so laughed it off, and in such a way that my victory was not really complete: the laugh was on his side" (p. 234). Such a minor triumph is the best the narrator can achieve, but it does provide some fuel for his romantic dream of conquering his companions with his stature and wit. His dream disintegrates when he arrives at the restaurant an hour early; his self-consciousness, his appearance, and the stares of the waiters reduce him to a frantic state by the time his acquaintances arrive. He proceeds to sink lower and lower under their disdainful glances. Several times he attempts to build himself up to one assertive action. "I'll go this minute!" he thinks. "But of course I remained." Later, pacing the room, he mentally threatens to sing, but naturally stays silent. Even his derisive toast to Zverkov and his threat of a duel with Ferfichkin provoke only laughter. Finally he grasps the last value of the underground, his separation from others. Abandoning all thoughts of action as he paces across the room, he thinks bitterly, "I walk up and down to please myself and no one can prevent me." But the Underground Man's consciousness will not let him assuage his pain with such meager consolation. He is excruciatingly aware of his impotence and his position, seeing it not only in relation to his companions but to his entire life:

> At times, with an intense, acute pang I was stabbed to the heart by the thought that ten years, twenty years, forty years

would pass, and that even in forty years I would remember with loathing and humiliation those filthiest, most ludicrous, and most awful moments of my life. (p. 250)

The dinner episode expands the Underground Man's knowledge of himself, but it offers no resolution to his paradoxical impotence. In fact, as he leaves to pursue the others to the brothel, his state of mind is strikingly similar to that portrayed in Part I of the novel. In Zverkov, as in the laws of rationalism, he has acknowledged an external force. He has tried to overcome that force and failed, but he refuses to be reconciled to that failure. He must follow the others to the brothel, thinking with a fascinating combination of irony and naïveté, "So that is it, this is it at last—contact with real life."

"Contact with life" is the theme of his relations with the prostitute Liza, the focal point of the confession of *Notes from the Underground.* In dealing with opposites like Zverkov, with whom he had nothing in common, the narrator was concerned only with his own ability to act. With Liza, on the other hand, he learns about himself through her. She too is sinking into a kind of underground hole, though she is barely conscious of it. The narrator sees the similarity and pities her. But his pity soon turns upon itself, producing a combination of tortured self-pity and cruelty toward the girl. At the end of his confessions to her, the hero finally achieves an understanding of himself and his relation to the external world.

The use of Liza as a mirror can be seen as an inevitable consequence of the underground psychology. After shutting himself off from the external world, the narrator can look only at himself. He cannot see the simple girl as a person with possibilities for good, but only as an object in which is reflected his own debased self. He has already performed this process of creating a mirror with his servant Apollon, who leers at him and reminds him of all the hateful aspects of his life. "It was as though he were chemically combined with my existence," he cries, "an integral part of that flat" (p. 282). Similarly, Liza becomes more and more entangled in the narrator's struggle to understand himself. But unlike the static, mocking reflection of the Underground Man in Apollon, the mirror in Liza is a tabula rasa. She is pliable and submissive, preparing to reflect whatever qualities the narrator reveals. Thus she leads him to his final horrible vision of himself, the climax of his confession.

The affinity between the narrator and the girl is established when he first attempts to talk to her. She brushes off his questions and lapses into silence, and he realizes how close her state of depression is to his own: "That answer meant, 'Let me alone; I feel sick, sad.' . . . God knows why I did not go away." In part, his decision to remain continues the compulsive self-flagellation that has pervaded all his actions on that evening; but it is clear that he is also drawn to the girl, both in a perverse delight at his power over her and in an attraction to a person who shares some of his feeling of degradation. He begins to lecture her.

The confession in the brothel is a patently false one, full of self-pity and romanticism. The narrator relishes the respect he can attain in her eyes—and through her, in himself. He inverts his views so flagrantly that he comes to epitomize the moralist–rationalist philosophy which the entire novel derides: "Such a thing, Liza, happens in those accursed families in which there is neither love nor God. . . . Another thing, Liza, man is fond of reckoning up his troubles, but does not count his joys" (pp. 264–65).

Several times he feels real emotion amid these blatant lies, but he always withdraws from it. "Damn it all," he thinks at one point, "this is interesting, this is kinship!" But in the next line he laughs, "It was the game that attracted me most" (p. 262). Later, when he again approaches sincere feeling, he is seized by the thought, "What if she were suddenly to burst out laughing?" He quickly retreats again. When he has avoided all possibilities for affection or understanding, only his awful cruelty remains:

> I had felt for some time that I was turning her soul upside down and rending her heart, and—and the more I was convinced of it, the more eagerly I desired to gain my objective as quickly and as effectually as possible. It was the exercise of my skill that carried me away. (p. 272)

The narrator leaves Liza in a state of abject despair and bestows on her, as if from far above, an invitation to visit him.

As soon as he returns to his home, however, he loses his feeling of power and composure. He becomes obsessed with the thought of her visit, with the idea of her seeing his way of living. At times he twists his apprehension into a bold dream in which he is the girl's compassionate "savior"; then he sinks into a dark hatred of her. After his feeble effort to assert himself by withholding Apollon's salary, the narrator even blames Liza's influence for that. It is clear that, in her passive manner, she has moved him greatly; she has shown him something of himself. By the time Liza does come, he has stripped his soul bare. He is ready for his most honest effort at self-discovery.

The scene in his own lodging is an inversion of the lies of the narrator's confession in the brothel. The benign thoughts about love and joy are shattered in the admission that "I was incapable of love, for I repeat, with me loving meant tyrannizing and showing my moral superiority." When he had left her the first time, "She was lying on her face, thrusting her face into the pillow and clutching it in both hands." Now the narrator himself is in tears, "lying face downward on the sofa with my face thrust into the nasty leather pillow" (p. 291).

This carefully constructed inversion of ideas emphasizes the repetitive nature of all of the Underground Man's confession. He covers the same ground time and again, achieving more perception incrementally rather than in a single redemptive moment. Therefore, after he pours out his hateful opinion of himself, he can find no new truth or satisfaction in his confession. Instead, he reverts to his petty, obsessive cruelty, screaming at her: "And for what I am confessing to you now, I shall never forgive you either!" In his increasing involvement with Liza, the narrator feels an emotion as complex as his view of his own existence: "How I hated her and how I was drawn to her at that minute!" His confession, ironically, has produced only a new paradox in his tormented consciousness.

In the events he remembers, the Underground Man finds little but shame and paradox. Yet when he ends his confession, he is a different man. His confession to Liza has brought him no justification, but it has served a crucial purpose. His false morality and romanticism are purged from his soul, leaving a clear perception of the paradoxes and the "wall" which enclose his life. Having failed to find a defense for his underground existence, he finally stops seeking one. He no longer struggles hopelessly with the paradoxes of his existence, but actually affirms them. Out of his accumulated failures to deal with others, the Underground Man has created a vision of a dark community of all men, each imprisoned in his own underground by the same inevitable wall of reason. By his own acute suffering and awareness, the hero has naturally earned a preeminence in such a world:

> I have only carried to an extreme in my life what you have not dared to carry halfway, and, what's more, you have taken your cowardice for good sense, and have found comfort in deceiving yourselves. So that perhaps, after all, there is more life in me than you. (p. 297)

The bitter triumph of this extraordinary passage shows more than an effort by the narrator to ease his own suffering by transferring it to others. It is also an impassioned statement of the Underground Man's "will," which enables him to reject the world so completely. Frederick Hoffman has described the Underground Man's defiant speeches as a process of "expedient self-abasement," which affirms his being even amid the lowest degradation of his life:

> He is in the act of asserting a superior inferiority, one of the many paradoxes by means of which he nourishes his identity. Dostoevsky wants, here and throughout, to describe a condition of extreme self-willing, a flagrant violation (and at the same time an exploitation) of reason and propriety. . . . The point is that the Underground Man *wills;* however distorted and ingeniously tortured (and comical) his postures and gestures are, they are willed; they are not rational or logical or predictable.[3]

Like everything else in the Underground Man's confession, the affirmation of this final vision is left somewhat ambiguous, shaded with doubt. In part, it is illusory, like the pleasure he finds in brushing shoulders with the officer on the Nevsky. Robert L. Jackson suggests this negative element:

> The Underground Man is not defending his freedom, but protesting his enslavement, his permanent condition of abasement. But through sustained protest, through "malice" his refusal to recognize the right of the forces humiliating him, he gains the illusion of freedom—a negative victory that is, indeed, the difference between self-recognition and extinction.[4]

There is something beyond self-delusion, however, in the vision at the end of *Notes from the Underground.* There remains a clear consciousness of the narrator's own role and of the world he defies.

3. Hoffman, *Samuel Beckett,* p. 6.
4. Jackson, *Dostoevsky's Underground Man,* p. 48.

The notes begin with many self-conscious references to the reader, which disappear as the narrator becomes more engrossed in his confession. At the conclusion, he returns his attention to the reader, united with him in a new and profound manner. Momentarily abandoning the total alienation he has sought, the Underground Man delivers his piercing indictment of weak mankind, a race capable only of slavery or the underground. Having examined himself so closely in his confession, he is able to taunt both the reader and himself with the awesome nature of the freedom he has tried to affirm: "Come, try, give any one of us, for instance, a little more independence . . . relax the control . . . I assure you we should be begging to be under control again at once" (p. 297).

Nevertheless, freedom is far more attractive to the Underground Man than the universal effort "to try to contrive to be some sort of generalized man." He pledges himself to his perpetual rebellion against the wall of reason, and his glimpse of the danger of limitless freedom remains as an indication of the tragic possibilities of the underground mentality—possibilities to be more fully explored in his spiritual heirs, such as Raskolnikov and Ivan Karamazov.

Notes from the Underground is a seminal novel for the development of Dostoevsky's great works. It consolidates his antirationalist philosophy and his total rejection of the optimism and determination which would render man incapable of tragedy. The importance of Dostoevsky's philosophical decision can scarcely be overestimated; Eliseo Vivas goes so far as to say: "It is his antirationalism which is the source and head of all his insights and attitudes, theological, psychological and political."[5]

5. Eliseo Vivas, "The Two Dimensions of Reality in *The Brothers Karamazov,"* rep. in René Wellek, ed., *Dostoevsky: A Collection of Critical Essays* (Englewood Cliffs, N.J., Spectrum [Twentieth Century Views Series], 1962), p. 88.

The world-view at the end of *Notes from the Underground* recalls Augustine's cry that "every man is a liar,"[6] with its implication that truth must be sought in theological terms. The psychological impact of the problem of freedom and responsibility is also felt on the author's later work. Finally, his unsparing portrayal of "liberal" types indicates Dostoevsky's fidelity to the underground political view.

Every dark and evil Dostoevskian hero who follows the Underground Man bears some imprint of his metaphysic; Jackson places him at the center of the development of the author's characters:

> The Underground Man occupies a transitional position in Dostoevsky's works: he represents in part the culmination of Dostoevsky's study and defense of the "little man," and he represents as well the beginning of Dostoevsky's critical examination of the anti-hero and social apostate. It is in the Underground Man that the timid rebellion of Devushkin takes on the destructive character that Dostoevsky will condemn in Raskolnikov.[7]

As such a pivotal figure, the Underground Man leaves a rich legacy, including the concept of the negative anti-hero and the philosophy which leads to Ivan Karamazov's "all is permissible." One aspect of this legacy is the idea of confession as the means of baring the character's soul.

As has been noted, the technique of confession did not originate in Russia with Dostoevsky. Partly due to the influence of the church, it was a favorite form of several of his predecessors. Dostoevsky's great achievement was to take this well-known custom and examine all its psychological and philosophical possibilities. The confession of the Underground Man is brilliant not because it shows us who he is, but because it reveals his

6. St. Augustine, *Confessions,* p. 337.
7. Jackson, p. 49.

motivations and compulsions and portrays the process of a man learning for himself who he is.

In his longer novels, Dostoevsky chose to abandon the first-person narrative, but this does not reflect any lessening of his concern with the confessional form. Philip Rahv points this out in regard to *Crime and Punishment,* written within two years of *Notes from the Underground:*

> He had written a complete draft of the novel in the form both of a diary and a murderer's confession. These versions turned out to be so unsatisfactory, chiefly because of the cramping effects of the method of narration in the first person, that he was forced to scrap them.[8]

However, these considerations did not prevent Dostoevsky from dealing with the confessional impulse throughout his later work. "The notion of confession," Gide notes with admiration, "comes up again and again, almost with the quality of an obsession, in Dostoevsky's novels."[9] An analysis of only a few of his many confessional characters will illuminate Dostoevsky's enormous role in formulating the genre of the modern confessional novel.

Although it contains no single confessional hero of the intensity of the Underground Man, *Crime and Punishment* is a monumental exploration of the possibilities of confession. The alternative of confession is always with Raskolnikov, offering to free him of his burden of guilt. At the same time, through his sporadic confessions to himself, Raskolnikov desperately attempts to clarify his own motive for the crime.

Part of the genius of *Crime and Punishment* lies in the author's combination of the compulsion to confess with a tonal manipulation which avoids the unaltered gloom of the underground.

---

8. Philip Rahv, "Dostoevsky in *Crime and Punishment,*" rep. in Wellek, ed., p. 23.

9. André Gide, *Dostoevsky* (Norfolk, Conn., New Directions, 1961), p. 79.

Raskolnikov is surrounded by stories of confession; some are grotesque almost to the point of being humorous, yet they serve the purpose of maintaining the idea of this alternative for the hero. The most comical of these stories is the "over-confession" of Marfa Petrovna Svidrigailov, whose efforts to reestablish Dounia's reputation lead her into a ritualistic recitation of her letter in every house of the town. "She was busy for several days in driving about the whole town," writes Raskolnikov's mother, "because some people had taken offense through precedence having been given to others."[10]

"Funny fellow!" says the innkeeper as Marmeladov begins his confession to Raskolnikov. But the words of this strange and pitiful man quickly fade from humor into horror; he is the embodiment of the intense self-humiliation of the Underground Man. For this weak man who has lost all control of himself and perpetrated the most dire injustices on his family, all that remains is the malignant pleasure of confession. Unlike the Underground Man, however, Marmeladov is unable to achieve even the most deluded self-affirmation, which might allow him to turn on his listeners and assert some justification for his life. He can only plunge on through the depths of his acute suffering, until he finally sees himself as a Christ-figure, a prototype of suffering: "I ought to be crucified, crucified on a cross, not pitied!" Marmeladov sees only one side of this image, however, and remains a ludicrous parody of Christ, experiencing pain and suffering without any hope of finding redemption or meaning in it. He even rejects the posture of defiance which helps sustain the Underground Man, saying, "I accept it all, not with contempt, but with humility" (p. 18).

Marmeladov's existence, like that of the Underground Man and Raskolnikov, is outside the "rational" world; but he lacks

10. Fyodor Dostoevsky, *Crime and Punishment,* trans. Constance Garnett (New York, Avon, 1956), p. 33. (Henceforth quotations from this novel will be identified by page numbers in parentheses.)

the spirit of rebellion and the grand idea of rising above the world which distinguish those two heroes. His self-alienation is a result not of free will but of weakness; his suffering is inextricably confused with its cause. "The more I drink the more I feel it," he says. "I drink so that I may suffer twice as much!" (p. 19) Lacking the free will to control his own confession, Marmeladov can gain no perception from it. His self-humiliation leads only to the ironically unproductive confession on his deathbed: "The confession was soon over. The dying man probably understood little" (p. 145).

Marmeladov's compulsive, hopeless confession plays an important role in Dostoevsky's development of the hero of *Crime and Punishment*. Raskolnikov is at once fascinated and terrified by the stranger's tale of painfully contradictory emotions, which seem to reflect the turbulent state of his own mind:

> The tavern, the degraded appearance of the man, the five nights in the hay barge, and the pot of spirits, and yet this poignant love for his wife and children bewildered his listener. Raskolnikov listened intently but with a sick sensation. (p. 23).

It is this strange attraction which draws Raskolnikov to the Marmeladov family after the man's ignominious death and leads to his involvement with Sonia, whose combination of holiness and prostitution offers a similarly alluring paradox. In fact, it is Sonia who ultimately provides Raskolnikov with his only answer to the haunting question which her father asks him in the tavern, "Do you understand, sir, do you understand what it means when you have absolutely nowhere to turn?" (p. 20)

Raskolnikov approaches the idea of confession for two reasons, neither of which resembles Marmeladov's desire for self-humiliation and suffering. A formal confession to the authorities offers him the possibility of alleviating the almost unbearable guilt which follows his crime. An internal confession, a sincere self-examination, offers hope of an answer to his painful questions about "what was wrong with his system." His determination to achieve knowledge by himself ultimately leads to a rejection of the first alternative and an increasing effort to embrace the second. Raskolnikov's confession thus focuses on a particular aspect of the Underground Man's consciousness—the possibility of justifying one's existence.

The manner in which the hero sees his own problems in Marmeladov's confession foreshadows Dostoevsky's use of mirrors or doubles throughout the novel. Although the idea of confession pervades Raskolnikov's consciousness, it is most fully articulated in three beautifully wrought scenes—two meetings of the hero and Sonia, separated by his interrogation at the office of Porfiry Petrovitch. This technique by which the hero sees himself through others is inherited from *Notes from the Underground* and becomes one of the enduring characteristics of the confessional novel. These three scenes constitute a triumph in this method, presenting a balanced picture of the possibilities of good and evil in man and in his confession.

Raskolnikov's first visit to Sonia is a striking parallel to the Underground Man's first meeting with Liza. He shies away from his own guilt and concentrates on torturing her. To her profound dismay, he predicts that her mother will die of consumption ("It will be better if she does") and that her sister will also become a prostitute. Echoing the Underground Man's words to Liza, he cries, "Tell me how this shame and degradation can exist in you side by side with other opposite, holy feelings? It would be better, a thousand times better and wiser to leap into the water and end it all!" (p. 248) Raskolnikov abandons this attitude only after he forces Sonia to read to him from the Bible, fully aware that he is torturing her by making her reveal "all that was her own." In the story of Lazarus he sees, by contrast, the hopelessness of his own position as an unbelieving murderer; but Sonia's "triumph and joy" as she reads it carry a new message of hope and a vision of the breadth of her soul. When she stops, Raskolnikov finally tries to confess, "I came to speak of something."

At this point, however, he cannot face confession and lapses into a speech reminiscent of the Underground Man's platitudes to Liza. It is a recitation of his earliest motives, which he has now so painfully refuted; it is an extension of the underground rationale, but one which no longer has relevance for Raskolnikov: "What's to be done? Break what must be broken, once for all, that's all, and take the suffering on oneself. What, you don't understand? You'll understand later. . . . Freedom and power, and above all, power" (p. 254). Sonia finds out little about her complex friend from all this, nor does Raskolnikov learn anything about himself. The primary function of this scene is its revelation of Sonia as the ideal person to whom he can ultimately confess. He leaves, but will keep his promise that "I'll tell you who killed Lizaveta."

The interrogation at Porfiry Petrovitch's the following day is a brilliant counterpoint to the two scenes with Sonia which it divides. It substitutes cleverness for compassion and rivalry for affinity. In contrast to Sonia, Porfiry is so devious that Raskolnikov cannot determine when he is being sincere and when he is trying to trick him. Fear dominates the interview.

The mirror in Porfiry Petrovitch might be compared to a hideous, shifting carnival mirror, reflecting Raskolnikov's own ideas in terrible caricature, then always moving before the student can locate the meaning of the image. Porfiry pretends to ridicule his own weapon, "this damnable psychology," and says ironically, "I'm a candid man." His professed candor leads him to a confession of his own, an inversion of that which he seeks from his victim. He even seizes one of Raskolnikov's favorite images, Napoleon, in a light-hearted reference ridiculing the philosophical basis of Raskolnikov's action: "I ought to have been in the army, upon my word I ought. I wouldn't have been a Napoleon, but I might have been a major, he-he-he!" (p. 262)

His perversion of all the possibilities of value in a confession deeply affects Raskolnikov, who seems on the verge of breaking down when the painter Nikolay breaks in with his own confession of the crime. The hero has been shaken and nearly defeated by Porfiry's "psychology which cuts both ways." He sees the vast potential for evil in a twisted confession such as Porfiry's, the false construction of the rational man.

Raskolnikov's second visit to Sonia and his confession to her reflect in microcosm much of the hero's internal conflict throughout the novel. One aspect of it is particularly significant in understanding Dostoevsky's concept of confession. As he prepares to see Sonia, Raskolnikov is almost bitter toward her, wondering about the limits of her compassion: "Well, Sofya Semyonovna, we shall see what you'll say now!" This concern with the effect his confession will have on others has characterized most of the hero's attempts thus far; he has been unable to concentrate on gaining a clear vision of his motives for himself. In his talk with Sonia, however, a great change takes place. After telling her of the crime, he tries to explain his desire to be a Napoleon, and she fails to comprehend. Then suddenly and dramatically, he casts away his cold theory in which human beings can be seen as mere lice: "But I am talking nonsense, Sonia . . . I've been talking nonsense a long time. That's not it, you are right there. There were quite, quite other causes for it!" (p. 315)

Raskolnikov proceeds to rake back over his consciousness, seeing his own sulkiness and strange nature at the base of his philosophy and tracing the growth of his burning need to achieve strength through daring. He sinks into "a sort of gloomy ecstasy," in which "he no longer cared whether she understood him or not" (p. 316). He has achieved his own personal perception.

The solution Sonia offers him is religious—to bow down, give himself up, expiate his sin. "We will go to suffer together," she begs, "and together we will bear our cross!" Rodya is moved; he reaches out to accept her little copper cross, but he suddenly draws back. Like Dmitri Karamazov admitting he is "not ready" to perform his "hymn of suffering" for the babe in his dream, Raskolnikov hesitates to join Sonia in her religion. He will not give himself up, but rather insists, again like Dmitri, in playing out the result of his action to the final limit. The importance of the scene hinges less on Sonia's alternative, however, than on the vision of himself which Raskolnikov achieves in his confession and the communion he feels with Sonia. It is hardly conceivable that the simple girl ever grasps his philosophical vacillations, yet she enables him to comprehend them clearly for himself for the first time.

It is characteristic of Dostoevsky and of all modern confessional novelists that the perception achieved by the hero remains ambiguous and elusive, far from the Christian ideal of total absolution and redemption. It is interesting that Dostoevsky's closest approach to such a redemptive vision, the epilogue of *Crime and Punishment,* produces the weakest section of that brilliantly sustained work. Rahv seems justified in his assertion that the epilogue's "hope and belief play havoc with the imaginative logic of the work."[11]

Ultimately, we must reject the conclusions of that unfortunate addition to the novel, in which Raskolnikov, imprisoned in Siberia, finally accepts the submission and religious hope from which he had retreated in Sonia's room. His change of heart is inexplicable, because his perception has not changed; his view of the meaning of crime remains clouded, and what passes as a seed of new hope is little more than bitter regret:

> "Well, punish me for the letter of the law. . . . Of course, in that case many of the benefactors of mankind who snatched power for themselves instead of inheriting it ought to have been punished at their first steps. But those men succeeded and so *they were right,* and I didn't, and so I had

11. Rahv, "Dostoevsky," p. 17.

no right to have taken that step." It was only in that that he recognized his criminality, only in the fact that he had been unsuccessful and had confessed it. (p. 410)

In the final line of the novel, Dostoevsky promises a new story (which he never wrote) to describe his hero's "gradual regeneration." And a complete new novel would be necessary to do this, because *Crime and Punishment* leaves its hero with only a thread of the vast fabric of hope which regeneration implies. The limitations on Raskolnikov's perception are emphasized most strongly immediately after his confession to Sonia. His "gloomy ecstasy" has brought him understanding, but it cannot purge him of his suffering; he realizes this with "a strange and awful sensation": "On his way to see Sonia he had felt that all his hopes rested on her; he had expected to be rid of at least part of his suffering, and now, when all her heart turned toward him, he suddenly felt that he was immeasurably unhappier than before" (p. 319). This feeling illuminates an important trait of the confessional novel. Although by its very nature confession offers the hero a hope of perception and new meaning, it cannot bring the modern hero the feeling of happiness and redemption which it provided for many traditional confessional figures. Such values can find no place amid the doubt, paradox, and passionate self-scrutiny of the Underground Man and his successors.

Crime and Punishment in its entirety does not subscribe to the characteristic forms of the confessional novel. It is told in a tightly constructed narrative rather than through the reflections of a man looking back on his life. Its scope ranges over many characters instead of concentrating exclusively on the hero and his internal struggles. And although the importance of confession in depicting Raskolnikov has been discussed, it should be noted that some crucial aspects of his character are revealed through symbols rather than conscious confession; two meaningful symbols which are more fully understood by the reader than by the hero are his dream of the peasants beating the helpless horse and his attraction for the invalid girl to whom he becomes engaged at one point. ("I really don't know what drew me to her," he admits of the latter case.)

Despite these qualifications, however, *Crime and Punishment* is a major contribution to the development of the confessional novel. In it, Dostoevsky explores the nature of guilt and the compulsive forces which lead to confession, as well as the relevance of confession to the tormented and confused hero. Marmeladov and Raskolnikov expand the concepts of self-abasement, suffering, and defiance of the rational world which are introduced in *Notes from the Underground.* Out of the broad and tumultuous sufferings of these figures, one clearly definable point emerges— the enduring importance of the self-scrutinizing consciousness in Dostoevsky's world.

Irving Howe has said of Dostoevsky, "He *exhausts* his characters, scours all the possibilities of their being."[12] This statement also applies to Dostoevsky's treatment of ideas. Hence, he never ceases to expand and explore the concept of confession, examining the spiritual heirs of the Underground Man. His short stories were particularly apt vehicles for experiments in confessional writing, because they allowed a return to the first-person narrative which the scope of his great novels forced him to abandon. Perhaps the most successful short story of this type is "A Gentle Spirit" (1876).

This story is actually an inverted confession, in which the narrator attempts to escape from his painfully clear understanding of himself through a process of self-delusion. Unlike the Underground Man, the narrator of "A Gentle Spirit" is immersed in affairs of the world, operating a pawnshop and hoarding money. He is plagued by the memory of a dishonorable discharge from

12. Irving Howe, "Dostoevsky: The Politics of Salvation," rep. in Wellek, ed., p. 70.

the army, which represents all the corruption within him and infects his mind with the paradoxes of the underground. Thus he becomes aware of the humiliating aspects of his occupation and grows almost paranoiacally defensive about it, declaring, "I was revenging myself on society, I really was, I was, I was!"[13] He is arrogant and anxious to show his superiority over the young girl who is to become his wife, yet feels compelled toward self-humiliation; in his proposal to the girl he even seeks to unite these opposing instincts:

> I frankly declared, without the least embarrassment, that, in the first place, I was not particularly talented, not particularly intelligent, perhaps not particularly good-natured, rather a cheap egoist (I remember that expression, I thought of it on the way and was pleased with it) and that very probably there was a great deal that was disagreeable in me in other respects. All this was said with a special sort of pride. (p. 553)

At one point the narrator admits that his marriage is based solely on a desire to rebuild his crumbling ego: "The feeling of inequality was very sweet, was very sweet." He takes special joy at being "an enigma" to the girl, since he himself is tortured with an all-too-clear vision of his condition.

The pawnbroker's effort to bring order to his life through his marriage is doomed when his young wife hears from other people about his past disgrace. As he recalls this nadir of his own degradation, he smothers any possibility of real confession in bitter self-delusion: "Well, I will tell the truth, I am not afraid to face the truth; it was *her fault, her fault!*" (p. 562) This is reminiscent of the Underground Man's tirade at Liza after his confession, but

13. Fyodor Dostoevsky, "A Gentle Spirit," trans. Constance Garnett, included in Phillips, William, ed., *The Short Stories of Dostoevsky* (New York, Dial, 1946), p. 553. (Henceforth quotations from this story will be identified by page numbers in parentheses.)

it is not followed by a perception similar to that achieved in *Notes from the Underground*. The pawnbroker continues to resist the truth about himself, and the "gentle spirit" in his wife rises up in revulsion against him, until the climactic scene in which she stands over his bed with the revolver. Unaware that he has seen her approach, the girl stands over the bed, summoning the will to kill her husband. He opens his eyes momentarily, closes them again, and awaits death. Finally, she turns away.

This dramatic confrontation seems to offer an ideal opportunity for a regeneration of self-respect and understanding in the hero; he has stared at death without flinching and survived to enter life once again. He even hints that the experience has recaptured the essential value he lost long before in the army: "I knew with the whole strength of my being that there was a struggle going on between us, a fearful duel for life and death, the duel fought by the coward of yesterday, rejected by his comrades for cowardice" (p. 570). When the climax passes, however, there is neither perception nor reconciliation. "She was conquered but not forgiven," the narrator gloats. The girl is stricken with brain fever, and the hero revels in his dark triumph, a new assertion of his superiority over her.

Gradually, however, his conquest fades; he realizes that his wife has withdrawn completely from him, instead of being attracted by the affirmation of his courage in the revolver incident. In her passivity, she attracts him more and more, until he finally forces his confession upon her with typical Dostoevskian fervor: "I was in too great a hurry, too great a hurry, but a confession was necessary, inevitable—more than a confession!" (p. 582) But on the brink of perception, the pawnbroker draws back; pride still counterbalances humility, and delusion still subverts honesty:

> I saw it all, all, to the smallest detail, I saw better than anyone; all the hopelessness of my position stood revealed. I told her everything about myself. . . . Oh, of course I changed

the conversation. I tried, too, not to say a word about certain
things. (p. 583)

After the girl's suicide, he engages in his most sincere effort
at self-examination. At last he faces the painful reality of his
army discharge and admits that "the gloomy past and my ruined
reputation fretted me every day, every hour" (p. 574). He even
appears ready to accept responsibility for his wife's death: "I
worried her to death, that's what it is!" But characteristically,
Dostoevsky does not allow his hero to become fully transformed.
We are permitted only a momentary glimpse through the delusions which cloud the narrative, before the hero reverts to his
evasive stance, calling the death a "misunderstanding" rather
than an act of will. When he returns home to find his wife's body
lying in the front yard amid a crowd of onlookers, his first thought
is, "The worst of it was they were all looking at me."

Thus, the story ends on a note of self-conscious shame rather
than purgation. The narrator has looked upon the truth and shied
away from it, accepting only part of his guilt. Dostoevsky has
presented a unique form of confession—one wrung from the narrator almost in spite of himself. When it is over, the pawnbroker
sinks into a mood of despair and alienation: "Men are alone—
around them is silence—that is the earth! . . . When they take
her away tomorrow, what will become of me?" Here, through
the mouth of a proud and self-deluding man of the world, comes
a distinct echo from the underground.

In *A Raw Youth,* Dostoevsky renews his earlier efforts to construct an entire novel with first-person narration. The novel is not
confessional, however, since the narrator, Arkady Dolgoruky, is
primarily concerned with learning the secrets and mysteries of his
father, Versilov, rather than of himself. The least highly regarded
of the major novels, *A Raw Youth* is often placed closer to Dostoevsky's journalistic works, such as *Diary of a Writer.* It is in-

teresting for its experiments with forms and images—such as the first-person narrative and the use of the double—which are refined and developed in other works. In the letter which the narrator receives from a tutor at the end of the novel, Dostoevsky indicates that he is as much intrigued with the potential of such a novel as with its achievement: "Such an autobiography as yours might serve as material for a future work of art, for a future picture of a lawless epoch."[14] Such an epoch finds its full realization in the author's final work, *The Brothers Karamazov*.

In the world of the Karamazovs, the Underground Man's dark vision of freedom is expanded to its ultimate limits. The heroes batter incessantly against the stone wall of rationalism, against the "Bernards" and Smerdyakov and Rakitin. In Dostoevsky's treatment of religion, as Berdyaev notes, "The tragic principle is victor over the principle of compulsion."[15] As the novel's various experiments in freedom scale new heights of tragedy, confessional techniques are frequently employed to illuminate the "great souls" of the characters. The author examines both false and sincere types of confession and presents new insights into the relation of the confessional genre to freedom and tragedy.

Father Zossima's discourse to his visitors as he approaches death is Dostoevsky's closest approximation to the traditional religious confession. The elder recounts only certain moments in his life, moments chosen for their value as a lesson to his listeners. His story includes three separate tales of sin and repentance— his brother Markel's, his own, and that of his "mysterious visitor" who turns out to be a murderer. From his speech arises a vision of the community of men, a world in which "every one of us is undoubtedly responsible for all men and everything on earth."[16]

14. Fyodor Dostoevsky, *A Raw Youth*, trans. Constance Garnett (New York, Macmillan, 1916), p. 560.

15. Nicholas Berdyaev, *Dostoevsky* (Cleveland, Meridian, 1962), p. 71.

16. Fyodor Dostoevsky, *The Brothers Karamazov*, trans. Constance Garnett (New York, Signet, 1960), p. 155. (Henceforth quotations from this novel will be cited by page numbers in parentheses.)

For a meaningful life in such a world, Zossima prescribes an all-embracing love and feeling of spiritual brotherhood.

The elder's idea of a universal guilt which can be assuaged only by God-directed love is one of the crucial thematic alternatives in the novel, though it is rejected in the chaotic explorations of individual guilt and free will in Ivan and Dmitri. Zossima's creed stands alongside the religious confessions of tradition, in contrast to the ultimate freedom proclaimed by Dostoevsky's modern confessional prototype, the Underground Man. "One's own free unfettered choice, one's own caprice, however wild it may be, one's own fancy worked up at times to frenzy—is that very 'most advantageous advantage' which we have overlooked," says the Underground Man (p. 201). Zossima sees such a preoccupation with total freedom as "a distortion of man's own nature": "The world has proclaimed the world of freedom, especially of late, but what do we see in this freedom? Nothing but slavery and self-destruction!" (p. 289) In seeing man's innate weakness, Zossima echoes the tradition of Augustine, who wrote, "No man is free from sin, not even a child who has lived only one day on earth."[17] For such a weak being, complete and unguided freedom can mean only destruction.

If one accepts this idea that man's freedom must be controlled, he faces the choice between Zossima's formula of love and the Grand Inquisitor's world of slavery. When Zossima bows down before Dmitri, the hero who is to probe the limits of freedom and suffering, he unites himself with Christ kissing the Inquisitor and Alyosha kissing Ivan; he affirms the necessity of some men to pursue freedom to its end, however destructive, and pledges himself to try and save them through his own prayer of universal love.

Because of its close relation to tradition, the confession of Zossima lies outside the modern confessional genre being de-

17. St. Augustine, *Confessions,* p. 27.

veloped in Dostoevsky. Its idea of universal guilt modulates the intense personal guilt which the confessional hero must feel. The elder's recollections are more exhortatory than self-searching; he learns nothing new about himself while he teaches the others. The one typically Dostoevskian element of this section is the aftermath, when "the breath of corruption" leaves a lingering doubt over the validity of Zossima's vision. The author's avoidance of commitment to Zossima's ideas at this point enables him to maintain the turbulent and chaotic tensions of a world with no definite values. Only in such a world can the efforts of the Karamazovs to understand their existence take on the proportions of tragedy.

The speech which Fyodor Pavlovitch Karamazov calls his "confession" stands in direct antithesis to traditional religious confession and to the discourse of Father Zossima. At the same time, it is equally distant from the impassioned confession of the Underground Man. It stands as a mockery of all real confession, a wild outburst which contains neither sincerity nor self-discovery. Fyodor's tirades are meant to be amusing, but they shock and repel his listeners; they are intended to hide his degradation, but they only accentuate it. Vivas cites the ultimate irony of the old man's distorted confession: "Fyodor's buffoonery discloses what it intends to cover, a sick soul consumed with the need to castigate itself."[18]

Fyodor Karamazov is reminiscent of Marmeladov in *Crime and Punishment* in his inability to resist destructive habits, his compulsive desire to tell others of his plight, and the lack of self-perception in his confession. Marmeladov's confession, however, is marked by a peculiar honesty which is totally absent from Fyodor's speeches. Marmeladov suffers deeply and never attempts to hide either his pain or its causes; old Karamazov, on the other hand, seeks to exaggerate his pain until it obscures the causes and

18. Vivas, "Two Dimensions of Reality," p. 78.

frees him of his responsibility and guilt. This insincerity irreparably separates Fyodor from Marmeladov and from Marmeladov's connection with the underground consciousness.

Characteristically, Zossima sees through the old man's buffoonery to the evil within and gently counsels him, "Don't tell lies." For a moment, the old man seems impressed; then he descends to new depths of falsehood in an effort to regain the respect of the others in the room: "Blessed man! . . . Do you think I always lie and play the fool like this? Believe me, I have been acting like this all the time on purpose to try you. I have been testing you" (p. 51). The supreme insolence of these words is accentuated by the irony of the proud Fyodor's following question, "Is there room for my humility beside your pride?" His twisted confession has completely inverted reality; the only true picture it exposes is that of the speaker's sick and evil soul.

During the chapter called "The Disgraceful Scene," Fyodor directly attacks the institution of religious confession in order to infuriate the priests. "Speaking from the confused memory of old slanders," he shouts, "Confession is a great sacrament, before which I am ready to bow down reverently; but there in the cell, they all kneel down and confess aloud. Can it be right to confess aloud?" (p. 89) This accusation emphasizes Fyodor's opposition to Zossima's creed and to the true confessional tradition, but it also illustrates the total perversion of reality in his thoughts. He criticizes open confession, which he has been practicing in his demented way for the entire scene, and praises its religious basis, which is completely foreign to him.

The sickness of Fyodor Karamazov's soul recalls in part the delusion of Katerina Ivanovna Marmeladov, who talks so much of her grandeur and her family connections that she comes to believe the myths. "He was so carried away by his own acting," we are told, "that he was for one moment almost believing it himself" (p. 91). Fyodor also employs the self-conscious literary allusions of Luzhin, the suitor of Dounia Raskolnikov, and of the narrator of "A Gentle Spirit." But the old man goes far beyond such minor weaknesses, into the depths of sensuality and depravity. He is sadistic, longing "to revenge himself on everyone else for his shortcomings," and fiercely proud, despite his attempt to appear humble. His confession, with its blatant falsity designed to cover rather than discover his soul, is a total perversion of the confessions of both religion and the underground.

In Zossima and old Karamazov, Dostoevsky presents opposite extremes of the non-confession. Essentially, the modern confession can be described as a quest for values, an effort to impose meaning and order on one's life. Because Zossima has long since chosen his principle of life, his confession becomes little more than a sermon, explaining his values but never questioning them. Fyodor Karamazov, on the other hand, lacks any conception of internal order and values and does not feel any desire to conceive of them. Both men thus fall short of the passionate, self-questioning introspection which is the hallmark of the modern confessional hero.

The "broad souls" of Ivan and Dmitri Karamazov gives Dostoevsky an opportunity to examine the possibilities of confession on a larger scale. Richard B. Sewall has defined the dominant mood of *The Brothers Karamazov* as "one of disorientation and search . . . as each of the brothers tries to find his center out."[19] This search for the center of the self clearly brings the Karamazovs into the forefront of any consideration of the development of confession in Dostoevsky's work.

The sporadic, reluctant series of confessions which reveal the internal life of Ivan Karamazov can hardly be classed with the single-purposed self-examination of the Underground Man as a prototype of the confessional form. Nevertheless, Ivan's process of self-discovery is the most brilliant application of Dostoevsky's novelistic virtuosity to a hero's confession. In its carefully con-

19. Sewall, *The Vision of Tragedy,* p. 109.

trolled structure and its ultimate refinement of the technique of the double, this hesitant and tormented confession is a monument in the literature of self-discovery.

The truth at the center of Ivan's existence is exposed to him in a series of agonized stages. The entire complex process can be roughly defined in three phases—intellectual, moral, and spiritual —each of which focuses on one aspect of the hero's condition in order to draw him closer to his terrible self-recognition. All three of these phases are united by the use of the double.

The idea of the double has been equated with that of the mirror, reflecting certain facets of the hero's existence and thereby accelerating his self-examination. This technique has already been noted in *Notes from the Underground* and *Crime and Punishment,* and it will be found in all confessional novels, as the hero seeks self-perception through his perception of others. However, Dostoevsky also saw the double as a more specific psychological phenomenon, an extreme schizophrenia symptomatic of a tortured and unbalanced mind. It is this meaning which he explores in the early novel, *The Double* (1846), and to which he returns in his treatment of Ivan Karamazov. This use of the double as a symptom of mental disorder is peculiarly apt for the portrayal of Ivan, who is so recalcitrant about facing his confession that he must be induced into self-discovery by forces beyond his conscious control. If he were able to control his doubles, he could withdraw from the guilt which they force upon him, simply turning away from the mirror images which they offered. Dostoevsky's only previous exploration of this type of strangely demonic double is found in *The Double.* In that work, the double which originates in the despondent consciousness of the hero gradually seizes complete control. The subjugation of the hero to his double is typified in one grotesque fantasy:

> Beside himself with shame and despair, the utterly ruined though perfectly just Mr. Golyadkin plunged headlong,

ready to go wherever fate might lead him; but at every step he took . . . there leaped up as though out of the earth, a Mr. Golyadkin precisely the same, perfectly alike and of a revolting depravity of heart. And all these precisely similar Golyadkins set to running after one another as soon as they appeared, and stretched in a long chain like a file of geese, hobbling after the real Mr. Golyadkin, so there was nowhere to escape . . . the whole capital was at last chock-full of duplicate Golyadkins.[20]

As Ivan Karamazov struggles through the three major parts of his confession, he experiences a fate similar to that of Golyadkin; the constructions of his own mind begin to elude his control. The Grand Inquisitor, center of his intellectual dialectic, is the main character in Ivan's "prose poem" and therefore subject to the will of his author. Smerdyakov, the bastard son of Fyodor Karamazov and spiritual son of Ivan, emulates the latter so intently that he too becomes Ivan's double. But in the moral phase of Ivan's confession, Smerdyakov breaks away from the hero's control and confronts him with their mutual guilt. Finally, Ivan faces the devil, a grotesque embodiment of all his "nastiest and stupidest thoughts." This version of Ivan's double is completely beyond his control and taunts him with the spiritual failure of his entire system.

Ivan's intellectual confession, which centers on "The Legend of the Grand Inquisitor," is essentially a peripheral approach. The setting is that of a religious confessional, as Ivan sits with the priestly Alyosha "in a place closed off by a screen." Initially, Ivan does turn his attention inward and tells of his love for Katerina and his conflict with Dmitri; then, as a warm rapport develops between the brothers, Ivan half-mockingly approaches "the eternal questions." He carefully maintains his separation from the Grand Inquisitor, attempting to stay on the periphery

20. Fyodor Dostoevsky, *The Double*, trans. Constance Garnett, included in *Three Short Novels*, pp. 115–16.

of self-examination. "I don't want to understand anything now," he says at the start of his "poem." "I want to stick to the facts. I made up my mind long ago not to understand" (p. 224). At the conclusion, he dissociates himself from the Grand Inquisitor in even stronger terms: "It's all nonsense . . . only a senseless poem of a senseless student."

These denials cannot be taken altogether seriously, however, because Ivan's legend clearly holds a strong influence over his mind. The Grand Inquisitor story might best be seen as a sort of vicarious confession, in which the hero takes a guarded, tentative step toward self-recognition. He has begun to comprehend the tremendous problems which freedom poses for man, and, in spite of himself, he feels an involvement with those problems. He seeks some hope in the "strength to endure anything . . . the strength of the Karamazov baseness," although he is unable to enthusiastically affirm that strength, as Dmitri does later. Finally, Ivan reaffirms his own position in regard to the problem posed in his legend, telling Alyosha, "The formula, 'all is lawful,' I won't renounce. Will you renounce me for that?" (p. 243) Alyosha's answer is the silent kiss which reflects Christ's gesture at the end of the legend—a striking assertion that Ivan is inextricably bound to the Grand Inquisitor story. Despite his cautious approach, Ivan's intellectual confession has drawn him within the periphery, into the beginnings of confession.

In the moral phase of his confession, Ivan is forced into much greater self-recognition. Before he finally accepts the guilt for his father's death, however, he resists with all his being. He listens with horror as his leering double, Smerdyakov, bestows mocking praise upon him and makes it clear that he considers himself a sort of physical tool of Ivan's mind. When Ivan went away on the night of the crime, Smerdyakov asks insinuatingly, "How could I help drawing conclusions?"

During their first two interviews, both the hero and his double hesitate on the edge of complete confession. Smerdyakov holds onto his legal alibis, and Ivan bolsters himself with the assurances of Alyosha and Katerina that Dmitri is the murderer. Finally, the storm of suffering and hatred within Smerdyakov compels him to confess, and the confession of Ivan's double simultaneously enunciates the guilt of Ivan himself: *"You* murdered him," Smerdyakov cries. "You are the murderer! I was only your instrument, your faithful servant, and it was following your words I did it" (p. 565).

Indisputably confronted with the reality of his guilt, Ivan ceases to flee it and, in recognizing it, achieves a momentary sense of meaning—the only real peace which his troubled mind ever enjoys. On his way home, he embraces and cares for the same peasant whom he had cruelly knocked down earlier in the day. He returns home with a firm resolution to accept the full burden of his guilt and save Dmitri.

Ivan's perception, however, is fragile, for "he was at that moment on the verge of an attack of brain fever." This vague disease heralds the end of his short-lived peace and the entrance of the devil, initiating the spiritual phase of Ivan's self-discovery. The devil expands Ivan's awareness beyond the guilt for the murder to an even more painful realization of all the shameful and meaningless elements of his life. Ivan hurls tea in his tormentor's face and curses him bitterly, but he is ultimately powerless as his "foundations"—including his resolution to save Dmitri—collapse beneath him.

As Smerdyakov had done, the devil expresses Ivan's confession through a confession of his own. "I have the same philosophy as you," he says. " 'All things are lawful' and that's the end of it." His derisive speech brings Ivan a fuller understanding of himself, but it is a grim understanding that is more destructive than purgative. After exposing the insubstantiality of the bases on which Ivan has built his life, the devil ridicules the idea that the hero might find new values with which to replace them. He claims that Ivan's lifelong rejection of the motives of virtue and conscience will make any subsequent attempt at confession meaningless; since pride is the only motive for such an act which Ivan has ever acknowledged, a confession at the trial would merely be a hollow effort to assuage that pride. Thus, the devil presents a powerful philosophical endorsement of the accusations first expressed by Ivan's other double, Smerdyakov: "You won't go to give evidence. . . . You won't want to spoil your life forever by taking such a disgrace on yourself" (p. 573). This indictment suggests that Ivan's bitter self-discovery has stripped him not only of his beliefs and his temporary perception, but also of all possibility of meaningful confession.

This bleak prediction is borne out with terrible finality in Ivan's desperate attempt to confess his guilt at the trial. For the first time Ivan initiates a confession himself, without the prodding of his doubles, and it fails miserably. The contradictions of his tortured mind drive him away from the facts into a demented account of his meeting with the devil; his testimony is discredited, and he is carried away as a madman. Dostoevsky compounds the irony of the situation by relating Ivan's failure directly to the decline of Dmitri's hopes; Ivan's speech incites Katerina to give the most damaging evidence of the entire trial. Thus, Ivan proves incapable of straightforward confession; the only self-discovery which he can adapt to his nature is the painful and destructive confrontation with his doubles, a brilliant variation on the consistent Dostoevskian theme of confession.

In contrast, Dmitri Karamazov's "Confessions of a Passionate Heart" are approached with all the compulsive fervor implied in their title. Even in the darkest moments of his turbulent life, Dmitri seems to see a promise of hope in confession. At the extremities of suffering and debauchery, he always feels he can set things right and restore his honor, and he expresses this emotion in exuberant self-revelation. Like Ivan, Dmitri begins his confessions by talking to Alyosha. "I must tell someone," he cries to his brother. "You are an angel on earth. You will hear and judge and forgive. And that's what I need, that someone above me should forgive" (p. 104). But this religious beginning proves as illusory as the setting of Ivan's confession. It soon becomes clear that Dmitri is far more concerned with suffering than with absolution. Unlike Ivan, he never hesitates to cite the basest motives behind all his acts and never tries to avoid blame, even when it appears that someone else might actually be at fault. In his impassioned embrace of suffering and degradation, Dmitri echoes the Underground Man.

The suffering of Dmitri Karamazov, however, is of far greater scope than that of the Underground Man. Dmitri is destined not only to feel it and think about it, but to act it out to its limits, plunging "heels up" toward its consummation. Dmitri's confessions are in large part technical devices by which Dostoevsky illustrates events from the past or premonitions about the future. Dmitri's intense adventure in suffering is predominantly acted out in the present, not confessed. "I want to live," says the Underground Man, "in order to satisfy all my capacities for life, and not simply my capacity for reasoning, that is, not one-twentieth of my capacity for life" (p. 203). Dmitri's life is so absorbed in affirming this facet of the underground rationale that he can no longer be confined by the method of the underground.

The various confessions which Dmitri blurts out during the novel are particularly noteworthy for the ironic misunderstandings which they produce. His frank confession to the police about "the old man and the blood" leads him to be suspected of the murder he didn't commit; then, in a misguided effort to be helpful, he almost seals his fate by honestly building up the case for his motive:

> I have never concealed my feelings. The whole town knows about it—everyone knows in the tavern. Only lately I de-

clared my feelings in Father Zossima's cell. . . . And the
very same day, in the evening I beat my father. I nearly killed
him, and I swore I'd come again and kill him. (p. 422)

On the other hand, the one confession which eventually might
have saved him—his chest-beating and whispering to Alyosha—
is uttered in mysterious and restrained terms which cloud its
meaning. Thus, rather than alleviating his suffering, Dmitri's
confessions serve to spur him toward his ultimate pain.

Dmitri is frustrated and enraged by the meticulous interrogation he undergoes at Mokroe. Impetuous and anxious to tell
everything, he cannot understand the officers' attention to details
or their efforts to pry further facts from him. When they finish, he
says, "I see that I am lost." Yet he also feels relieved of a burden;
when he sleeps, he dreams of a shivering "babe" and is overcome
with compassion for all those who suffer in the world. In a striking passage, he applies his turbulent Karamazov soul to the ideal
of Zossima:

> He wanted to do something for them all, so that the babe
> should cry no more, so that the dark-faced, dried-up mother
> should not weep, that no one should shed tears again from
> that moment. He wanted to do all this at once, at once, re-
> gardless of obstacles, with the recklessness of the Kara-
> mazovs. (p. 464)

For the first time he sees clearly the possibility of purgation: "I
accept the torture of accusation, and my public shame. I want to
suffer because by suffering I shall be purified" (p. 465).

During the trial and conviction, this vision leaves Dmitri,
forced out by the chaotic events and his own passionate outbursts.
It returns as he enters the prison hospital, talking of his determination to sing a "hymn from underground," a prayer for all
sufferers. But like Raskolnikov, he is "not ready" for such catharsis; he admits to Alyosha, "I wanted to sing a hymn; but if a guard

speaks to me, I will not have the strength to bear it . . . I am not fit for suffering" (p. 689). The final phrase seems partly ironic, since Dmitri has clearly proven himself eminently capable of suffering throughout the novel. It is meaningful, however, as a distinction between two types of suffering. He is truly "not fit" for the suffering preordained by Zossima's ideas and his vision of the babe. Dmitri is meant to experience only the vast range of suffering which he brings on himself, the suffering inevitable for the unbounded free will.

Although there is no confessional hero in *The Brothers Karamazov,* the novel presents a monumental selection of possibilities for and variations of the confessional form. Father Zossima links Dostoevsky to the religious tradition of confession. Ivan faces the realization of guilt and the self-destructive elements of confession. Dmitri carries the Underground Man's concern with suffering to new extremes and focuses on the possibility of purgation for the modern hero. In taking the Underground Man's philosophy to the testing ground of tragedy, Dostoevsky has expanded and further defined the genre of the modern confessional novel.

From the wide spectrum of Dostoevsky's characters, it is possible to identify certain consistent patterns which help to define the confessional genre. Dostoevsky maintains several characteristics of the traditional religious confession, most notably the need for honesty and sincerity on the part of the hero. Another basically religious aspect is the notion that, at some point, pride must give way to humility. Fyodor Karamazov's pride makes confession impossible, and pride keeps Raskolnikov and Ivan Karamazov from accepting the necessity of confession until late in their lives. On the other hand, the Underground Man sees himself as "a sick man . . . a nasty person, an imposter" and so plunges headlong into confession.

The first crucial element which Dostoevsky adds to the confessional tradition is that of the "overacute consciousness," in which the very act of thinking is painful and compels man to seek relief. Dmitri's awareness of his guilt is one example of this, but he seeks relief through action; the Underground Man, incapable of significant action, turns to confession. Closely related to this mood of compulsion is the confessional hero's unwillingness to accept his troubled existence as it is; he insists on a state of "perpetual rebellion," until he can find self-understanding.

An important difference between the Dostoevskian confession and earlier ones is in the abandonment of the concept of complete catharsis and purgation of guilt. Each of Dostoevsky's heroes ultimately retreats from a position of redemption. What remains is a fuller self-knowledge, a perception rather than a purgation. The hero is never saved or absolved by confession, but he does gain a vision of his "foundations" and his motives; he finds a meaning—however terrible—to sustain him in an otherwise meaningless world.

Several of the devices used by Dostoevsky become frequent tools of the confessional novelist. His use of other persons as mirrors of the self, his religious settings for confessions, and his many psychological realizations become integral to the modern confession. Freud, who later systematizes many of the brilliant observations of Dostoevsky (thus making them even more readily available to later writers), notes the importance of Dostoevsky's willingness to probe the criminal mind: "A criminal is to him almost a Redeemer, who has taken on himself the guilt which must else have been borne by others."[21] This capacity to see nobility even in evil opens the way to many modern confessions.

"Man is broad," Dmitri tells Alyosha, "too broad. I'd have him narrower" (p. 106). Svidrigailov speaks of a similar trait in his cynical words to Dounia Raskolnikov about her brother: "Russians in general are broad in their ideas, Avdotya Romanovna, broad like their land and exceedingly disposed to the fantastic,

21. Sigmund Freud, "Dostoevsky and Parricide," rep. in Wellek, ed., p. 108.

the chaotic. But it's a misfortune to be broad without a special genius" (p. 372). Dostoevsky's heroes are committed to the examination of their "broad souls," the search for the source of their own "special genius." The Karamazovs seek it in bold action or intellectual constructs or a religious faith. None of these paths are open to the Underground Man. Inextricably tangled with the world, he is at the same time impotent to "batter the wall" around him. His suffering turns inward, and confession becomes his special genius.

"For a long time," Berdyaev states, "European society had stayed at the fringes of being and was content with an outward existence."[22] When the narrator unites his own sickness with that of his readers at the end of *Notes from the Underground*, he declares such an outward existence to be impossible and leads man into a renewed concern with the self. This burning quest for self-discovery lies at the center of Dostoevsky's enormous contribution to the modern confessional novel.

22. This statement by Berdyaev is quoted by Sewall in *The Vision of Tragedy*, p. 107.

2. A DISINTEGRATED WORLD:

Gide,
Sartre,
and Camus

Even during his darkest examinations of the underground, Dostoevsky tempers the struggles of his confessional heroes with a certain hope. Although he continues to suffer, the hero of *Notes from the Underground* shows in the tormented accusations of his conclusion that he has at least been purged of falsehood and illusion. In Dostoevsky's subsequent novels, the heroes approach a more positive purgation, a possibility of regeneration of life. This possibility always eludes the hero, who is not ready to accept the necessary responsibility, but its enduring presence in the author's vision is frequently affirmed. The idea of purgation, retained by Dostoevsky from religious tradition, offers one principle of order in his broad and chaotic cosmos.

In the twentieth century, all such ordering principles have been called into question. Three major French novels—André Gide's *The Immoralist,* Jean-Paul Sartre's *Nausea,* and Albert Camus' *The Fall*—lead the confessional genre into a world which lacks even the fleeting and tentative approaches to purgation and perception that Dostoevsky's heroes experienced. Gide, Sartre, and Camus portray a world in which no values are firm, no regeneration is anticipated, and even basic personal relationships have become futile. They force their heroes to seek meaning in the only way that remains for them—intense self-examination. These heroes transport the Underground Man's idea of radical freedom into the world above the ground, extending that idea to its extreme limit. Ultimately, it turns upon itself, becomes twisted into forms which culminate in overwhelming guilt or utter meaninglessness, and finally produces a bitter, ironic echo of the original *Notes*—the confession of Jean-Baptiste Clamence in *The Fall.*

As all objective truth becomes hazy ("Don't lies eventually lead to truth?" asks Camus' hero), man is left to construct his own meaning for life. In *The Immoralist,* Michel turns to a Nietzschean code of power which leads to disaster; Roquentin, the narrator of *Nausea,* fails to distract himself sufficiently with his history studies and succumbs to the sheer awesomeness of existence; Clamence's proud materialism ends in a mocking and eternal laugh behind his back, and his "judge–penitent" role still fails to gain peace for him. For these heroes, confession is a hazy mixture of raw suffering, satire, and paradox. We are rarely sure when one of them is completely sincere, yet the overall effect of each confession is unequivocal—a vivid image of disintegration. Gide's hero expresses this pervasive theme: "Without a doubt, everything, in my life is falling to pieces. Nothing that my hand grasps can my hand hold."[1]

1. André Gide, *The Immoralist,* trans. Dorothy Bussy (New York, Vintage, 1958), p. 118. (Henceforth quotations from this novel will be identified by page numbers in parentheses.)

These three novels span more than half a century in the development of the modern confessional tradition. Their thematic relationships to one another and to Dostoevsky largely determine their selection here. Space limitations prevent discussion of Marcel Proust's massive experiments in subjective narration, as well as François Mauriac's largely confessional treatments of man's relation to God, although both these writers represent noteworthy derivations of the confessional genre in France. The sensitive prose of Rainer Maria Rilke's *Notes of Malte Laurids Brigge* (1910) and the psychological experiments of some of Maxim Gorky's stories, most notably *Karamora* (1924), should also be mentioned as significant confessional works which fall outside the somewhat arbitrary scope of this discussion.

A second qualification must be established before continuing. It is evident that the novels treated here are isolated from the total achievements of each of these vastly complex artists. *The Immoralist,* Gide's first novel, may be his finest, but can hardly be expected to expound his entire aesthetic vision. *The Fall,* which was Camus' final novel, is in several ways a sharp break from those that preceded it. It seems clear, therefore, that the critic must avoid any generalizations about the authors on the basis of these novels alone and must focus exclusively on their contributions to the confessional genre.

The Immoralist was published in 1902, *Nausea* in 1938, and *The Fall* in 1956. Many of the views of the authors are as widely divergent as this time lapse. The vision behind Gide's novel, as Brée and Guiton point out, "sees man as a being thrown into a world without any divine guidance or revelation, but with innumerable possibilities for 'becoming.' "[2] In contrast, the heroes of Sartre and Camus face an absurd world which severely limits such possibilities. A central theme in Gide's novel is the suppression of unconscious drives, while Sartre has denied the very

2. Germaine Brée and Margaret Guiton, *The French Novel from Gide to Camus* (New York, Harbinger, 1962), p. 26.

existence of the realm of the unconscious as described in classical psychoanalysis.[3] These are only a few of the numerous disagreements which separate these men, yet the existence of such differences makes the extraordinary similarities among their three confessional novels all the more striking.

These three authors owe a large mutual debt to Dostoevsky. Gide engaged in a detailed critical study of Dostoevsky and called him "the greatest novelist of all time." Two aspects of Dostoevsky's art have a particularly strong influence on *The Immoralist*. The first is the deep concern with confession; Gide wrote of Dostoevsky:

> The notion of confession, not murmured low into priestly ears, but made openly, before any and all, comes up again and again. . . . Characters are seized at certain moments . . . with the urgent desire to make confession, to ask pardon of some fellow-creature who often has not a notion of what it is all about, the desire to place themselves in a posture of inferiority to the person addressed.[4]

Secondly, Gide adopted Dostoevsky's "use of the 'imperceptive' or self-deluded narrator."[5] However, he also modified this device to an extent which reveals a crucial fact about the achievement of the French confessional novels. The delusion of Dostoevsky's heroes—as typified by the Underground Man at his lowest moments and the pawnbroker in "A Gentle Spirit"—is an effort to

3. In his introduction to "Existential Psychoanalysis," a section of *Being and Nothingness* which has been published separately (trans. Hazel Barnes, New York, Philosophical Library, 1953), Rollo May writes, "Sartre is constrained to deny the existence of 'the unconscious' because it merely offers man a subtle excuse for self-deceit or 'bad faith.' "

4. Gide, *Dostoevsky*, p. 79. In his introduction to this edition, Albert Guerard quotes a passage from Gide's *Journal* which indicates the value of this critical work in an evaluation of Gide as a novelist: "Everything I find means of saying through Dostoevsky," Gide wrote, "is dear to me. . . . It will be, just as much as a book of criticism, a book of confessions, to anyone who knows how to read; or rather, a profession of faith."

5. Albert Guerard, *André Gide* (New York, Dutton, 1963), p. 100.

shut out reality behind a screen of hysteria, obsessions, or asser-
tions of some imagined superiority. Michel is self-deluded (and
in his case the adjective "imperceptive" is far more fitting) in a
very different way. He keeps his conscious attention focused on
reality but fails to perceive the unconscious desires which he is
suppressing. Gide thus utilizes both Dostoevsky's narrative device
and contemporary psychological knowledge to cast new light on
the dark forces which Dostoevsky himself never ceased to explore.

Sartre was not as directly concerned with criticism and discussion of Dostoevsky as was Gide, but he was clearly influenced
by the Russian novelist. *Notes from the Underground* has been
termed "the best overture for existentialism ever written,"[6] and
it certainly had a far-ranging effect on Sartre's philosophy and
literature. In addition to its impact on Sartre's thought, Dostoevsky's novel also foreshadows elements in the narrative technique
of *Nausea*. One stylistic tool which is often employed in both of
these confessional novels is the sharp letdown—the sudden jolt
from romanticism or illusion into reality. The Underground Man
must time his "passionate desire to embrace humanity" so it falls
on a Tuesday, the only day on which he can visit his single friend.
Later, when he resolves to offer a grandiose apology to Zverkov
during the disastrous dinner party, he is cut off by Zverkov's derisive reply, "Insulted? *You* insulted *me?* Understand, sir, that you
never, under any circumstances could possibly insult *me.*"[7] This
ironic technique is often used by Roquentin, the narrator of
Nausea, to satirize the Autodidact and other people around him;
but the hero himself is not spared, as illustrated when he strives
vainly to reestablish some of the meaning of his past with Anny,
his former mistress:

> "Naturally, you don't remember the first time I kissed you?"
> "Yes, very clearly," I said triumphantly. "It was in Kew

6. Walter Kaufmann, ed., *Existentialism from Dostoevsky to Sartre*
(Cleveland, Meridian, 1963), p. 14. (The phrase is taken from Kaufmann's
introductory essay.)
7. Dostoevsky, *Notes from the Underground*, p. 251.

Gardens, by the banks of the Thames."
"But what you never knew was that I was sitting on a patch of nettles: my dress was up, my thighs were covered with stings."[8]

Albert Camus was as deeply concerned with Dostoevsky as was Gide and channeled his interest into philosophical rather than critical writings. *The Myth of Sisyphus* (1942) and *The Rebel* (1952), two of his major essays, deal at considerable length with the ideas of Kirilov in *The Possessed* and Ivan in *The Brothers Karamazov.* The confession of *Notes from the Underground* is the subject of both structural imitation and an ambiguous satire in *The Fall,* which also draws extensively from other sources in Dostoevsky. The manner in which emulation and satire interplay to create a brilliant new vision of the underground will serve as a crucial guide to the significance of Camus' novel in the confessional tradition.

In these novels, Gide, Sartre, and Camus have invented three heroes who share several significant common characteristics. All are intellectual, in education if not in attitude, and they often employ literary allusions. Antoine Roquentin, who meditates endlessly on the social history of various Bouville streets and dwells at length on de Rollebon, the elusive subject of the book he is unable to write, is the epitome of the "imbalance between internal and external things" which concerned Dostoevsky as he wrote *Notes from the Underground.* Overcome with an intense boredom, he is powerless against it; like the "overacute consciousness" of the Underground Man, his mind seizes every detail. Yet he is curiously cold, incapable of emotion except when faced with the thought of death or, finally, of existence. Thus, most of his journal wanders at the slow pace of a daydream. Its distinctive deadness is necessary to convey the extreme state of metaphysical nausea, the paradoxical condition of a man who

8. Jean-Paul Sartre, *Nausea,* trans. Lloyd Alexander (Norfolk, Conn., New Directions, 1959), p. 200. (Henceforth quotations from this novel will be identified by page numbers in parentheses.)

notices every detail of the scene whenever he enters a café, yet whose hand falls asleep while he is fondling a mistress.

Although he abandons his scholarship to seize a sensual creed which draws him irresistibly away from culture, the narrator of *The Immoralist* never loses his cold intellectual bearing as he tells his story. When he concludes his sordid tale, one of his listeners comments:

> He finished his story without a quaver in his voice, without an inflection or a gesture to show that he was feeling any emotion whatsoever; he might have had a cynical pride in not appearing moved, or a kind of shyness that made him afraid of arousing emotion in us by tears, or he might not in fact have been moved. (p. 145)

The speculation of Michel's friend is helpful in understanding the hero's nature, but it is far more noteworthy for its dramatic import. Michel's three friends perform a function similar to that of the three friends of Job, from whom they derive. They are "normal men," moderate, responsible, ordinary. Just as Job's visitors are unable to see the full meaning of the hero's stature or his tragedy, Michel's companions can only gasp at his revelations. They serve Gide by their implication of a certain uniqueness and stature in Michel, and, more important, their limited understanding testifies to the titanic nature of the struggle that has taken place within the hero.

The question, "Do you know . . .?" recurs throughout the narrative of *The Fall*, each time followed by a different literary allusion. As with Gide's use of Michel's friends, Camus' purpose in repeating this refrain goes far beyond the illumination of Jean-Baptiste's erudition. It continues to give the narrator and his listener more and more things in common and subtly draws the listener closer to the moment when the "I" of Clamence becomes a "we" and the demonic laughter envelopes another "guilty" soul. This ironic treatment of the intellectual eventually turns on the narrator himself, however, just as Roquentin cannot remain immune to the disdain he so casually directs at the Autodidact.

During his account of his sexual relations, Clamence exhibits the utmost detachment from his own sadism:

> I began, in fact, to mortify her in every way. I would give her up and take her back, force her to give herself at inappropriate times and in inappropriate places, treat her so brutally in every regard that eventually I attached myself to her as I imagine the jailer is bound to the prisoner. And this kept up till the day when, in the violent disorder of painful and constrained pleasure, she paid a tribute aloud to what was enslaving her. I have forgotten her since.[9]

Unlike Michel in *The Immoralist,* Clamence speaks of his cruelty in terms which are not only detached, but actually somewhat victorious. His cool detachment seems to emphasize his power. Only in his final words does his ironic power abandon him; then he is reduced to the desperate and deluded cry of a defeated man: "I am happy, I tell you, I won't let you think I'm not happy, I am happy unto death!" With all detachment and control stripped from him, the hero is seen to be suffering from the acute paroxysms of the Underground Man. The mocking laugh which echoes behind him is not only that of the girl on the bridge, but also, unmistakably, that of the master of irony, the author.

For Camus, this ultimate manipulation of his hero's tale, in which Clamence is forced, almost against his will, to reveal his inner suffering, maintains the distance between author and narrator. Such a separation is essential in the confessional novel, and Gide and Sartre also take pains to establish autonomy for their intellectual heroes. Gide achieves it by the "imperception" of Michel, as we have seen. Sartre faces a more difficult task be-

9. Albert Camus, *The Fall,* trans. Justin O'Brien (New York, Vintage, 1956), p. 65. (Henceforth quotations from this novel will be identified by page numbers in parentheses.)

cause Roquentin is concerned with the same philosophical problems as the author. Sartre's own use of irony achieves a measure of detachment, but he apparently feels a need to emphasize it, so he adds the very blunt device of the footnotes at the beginning of the novel, which imply an impersonal editor separating the hero from both the author and the reader.

The modification of the ideas of Dostoevsky and the development of a more intellectual hero are two ways in which Gide, Sartre, and Camus contribute to the confessional form. But the dominant philosophic impact of their respective confessional novels remains that of disintegration. Several concepts which emphasize and elaborate on that theme reappear throughout the works. The heroes feel a sense of isolation and the futility of human relationships; as their confessions progress, they suffer from the loss of any power to act meaningfully; and they are preoccupied with the problems of freedom and death.

An isolated narrator is one characteristic of all confessional novels, in the sense that he, like the Underground Man, tells his story "for himself alone." Every confessional hero is essentially alone when he makes his confession. Any people around him serve only as conventions, like a priest or judge in a religious or criminal confession, or as representatives of the world to which the hero may be attempting to relate. Michel's three friends serve in the former role, as does Alyosha Karamazov for Ivan and Dmitri; Clamence's companion in *The Fall* is the most striking example of the representative of the external world. But such figures are priests who cannot grant absolution, judges who cannot pass judgment. Any purgation or peace must come from within the hero and must be related to the world at large, not to any one companion.

The heroes of Gide, Sartre, and Camus extend the feeling of isolation beyond this basic idea. Like the Underground Man, they reveal that they have experienced it during much of the lives they speak about; they struggle constantly with the problems of separation from others and from their own pasts. This theme is treated most fully in *Nausea,* in which it becomes one of the most crucial and ironic aspects of the hero's disintegration. Roquentin's isolation begins with his pride; he rejects the society of others in the cafés and streets of Bouville because he feels that his active mind and vast experience are above trivial relationships. Much of his criticism of such people is the typical derision of an intellectual: "All these creatures spend their time explaining, realizing happily that they all agree with each other," he says. "In Heaven's name, why is it so important to think the same things all together" (p. 17). Soon, however, it becomes clear that his bitterness stems from a certain jealousy, a resentment that others are not burdened with the philosophical problems which plague him. As he satirizes them, he cannot help noting that they have solved the question of how to exist; of the men in the Café Mably, he says:

> Since they need a little luxury, they come here after their meals. They drink a cup of coffee and play poker dice; they make a little noise, an inconsistent noise which doesn't bother me. In order to exist, they also must consort with others. (p. 14)

During his lunch with the Autodidact at another café, he again derides those around him: "Each of them has his little personal difficulty which keeps him from noticing that he exists" (p. 150).

Roquentin's pride leads him to prefer his work and his own rich memories to such companions. But the genteel, witty de Rollebon grows elusive, difficult to approach, and, finally, boring; he gives up his book. As he sees his travels and "adventures" unconsciously parodied by the Autodidact and begins to feel only longing in his recollections of Anny, Roquentin realizes that he has also lost his memories: "You can't put your past in your pocket; you have to have a house. I have only my body: a man entirely alone, with his lonely body, cannot indulge in memories;

they pass through him" (p. 91). With these objects of his attention gone, Roquentin is forced to realize that he needed them as a shield against "the disgust of existing" just as much as others needed conformity or trivial problems. "M. de Rollebon was my partner," he admits. "He needed me in order to exist and I needed him so as not to feel my existence" (p. 133).

The irony of this discovery is compounded when he tries to regain contact with other people. His rendezvous with his former mistress is a miserable failure; Anny has, by her own admission, "outlived herself." The "perfect moments" she had always sought had proved as empty as the adventures which Roquentin had collected. Their relationship had been built on little "adventures," on delusions of meaningful action. Before he leaves her, Roquentin says, "One can't be a man of action."

The futility of all personal contact is illustrated further in the hero's meetings with the Autodidact. Throughout most of his journal, Roquentin is contemptuous toward this crude parody of the intellectual, who is doggedly ploughing through all the works in the library in alphabetical order. Yet after he abandons his book and begins to feel increasing pressure from his solitary existence, Roquentin is drawn to the Autodidact. "I needed to talk," he says of his acceptance of a luncheon invitation; but his acceptance indicates more. "The Sartrean intellectual wants to be judged," writes Victor Brombert. In Sartre's view, "we are all surrounded by mirrors, walled in by contradictory images of ourselves."[10] For such a hero, the mirror is an instrument not of self-discovery but of self-torture. He is "determined to find the most unflattering image of himself." It is this paradoxical dual need for companionship and humiliation which draws Roquentin into an attempt at communication with the Autodidact.

Inevitably, the attempt must fail. The crude intellectualism and

10. Victor Brombert, *The Intellectual Hero: Studies in the French Novel, 1880–1955* (Chicago, University of Chicago Press, 1964), pp. 188–89.

sentimental humanism of the Autodidact make him incapable of ever fulfilling or even understanding the complex needs within Roquentin. At first, his solicitation brings some comfort: "Someone is speaking to me, asking me if I am cold: I am speaking to another man: that hasn't happened to me in years" (p. 141). But his clumsy tale of how he loves all men as brothers repels Roquentin completely, and the meal ends with the hero's most violent attack of "the Nausea." Again, in his acute realization of his isolation from others, Roquentin is plunged from pride into humiliation. He is no longer able to look insolently on his ludicrous friend and abandons his superiority completely as he attributes his own growing self-hatred to the Autodidact; he credits the other with powers of subtlety and perception he had never before imagined:

> He has become respectful again, respectful to the tip of his toes, but in his eyes he has the ironic look of someone who is amusing himself enormously. He hates me. I should have been wrong to have any feeling for this maniac. (p. 160)

Roquentin has again achieved only the dark, self-flagellating side of his dual need; the other side, that of companionship and "finding a niche" in the world of others, has remained, as always, unattainable.

In Gide, the isolation of the hero follows a different course. At the outset of his story, Michel cuts himself off from the world; as he ruefully admits when he relates the circumstances of his marriage, "I pledged my life before I knew what the possibilities of life were" (p. 8). He marries Marceline to please his dying father. (It is a striking and revealing statement on Gide's view of love that it so often begins in the shadow of death, only to fade in less emotion-filled times. In *Strait Is the Gate,* Jerome's closest approaches to Alissa follow the deaths of his mother and aunt and the tragedy of her family's collapse.) The combination of the death of his father and his commitment to a girl who is a virtual stranger leaves Michel cut off from his moralistic upbringing, yet lacking any code with which to replace it.

The constant travels which comprise most of the physical action of *The Immoralist* present one of the crucial themes of the novel. They constitute a desperate effort to find what Roquentin called "a niche," a place in which the hero can relate himself meaningfully to the world. The symbol itself—constant motion in a search for stability—embodies the paradox and hopelessness of Michel's quest. Travel also hints at an escape, reflecting his constant flight from barely suppressed homosexual drives. Finally, it implies the fleeting nature of all values for the hero. He admires the orgiastic self-indulgence of the Roman prince Athalaric but cannot avoid the fact that it brought the boy death before he was twenty-one. Such is the fate of all the "possibilities of life" which Michel explores, including love itself. He admits this fact most directly in his account of the decline of love with Marceline— an account which he injects harshly into the memory of the first wonderful night on which he possessed her:

> But I believe there comes a point in love, once and no more, which later on the soul seeks—yes, seeks in vain—to sur- pass; I believe that happiness wears out in the effort made to recapture it; that nothing is more fatal to happiness than the remembrance of happiness. Alas! I remember that night. (p. 53)

Gide has thus brilliantly expanded the motif of the wanderer— traditionally a symbol of isolation—into a broad vision of the causes of that isolation in his hero.

As Michel struggles against his separation from other people and from the fullness of life, a second aspect of his isolation emerges. Roquentin loses his contact with the past; Michel finds himself unable to keep pace with the present. The youthful Charles, who provides so much joy on his Normandy farm, changes into a stuffy, educated man during an additional year of

66

30473

school and slips away from him. When he returns to North Africa, the boys who had delighted him have grown hard and cruel and lost their attractiveness. While the temporal world moves on, Michel indulges in a futile attempt to recapture past pleasures, retracing his steps through lands which have grown unrecognizable. This final journey completes his profound loneliness; unable to find any of the satisfactions he seeks in others, he simultaneously slips farther away from Marceline until the arduous and frustrated journey finally kills her. On his return to Biskra, once the scene of his deepest feelings of life, he asks, "What! Am I going to find here the same things I hated so at home?" (p. 137) The answer is inevitably affirmative; those "things" are within him, making relationships with others impossible.

The nature of Clamence's confession in *The Fall* precludes direct mention of any feeling of isolation. As he lures his listener into a community of guilt, he naturally attempts to appear at peace with that community. Nevertheless, his isolation is as important an element of irony in his story as it is in *Nausea*. During his successful life in Paris, Clamence always seeks high places. Although he appears in harmony with society, he is always striving to rise above others, to control them. This effort is typified in his attitude toward women: "For me to live happily it was essential for the creatures I chose not to live at all. They must receive their life, sporadically, only at my bidding" (p. 68). He admits that even his outwardly charitable acts are only attempts to gain more public admiration and thus to rise higher above other men. In his extreme pride, he sees himself as "half Cerdan, half De Gaulle," a perfect man; in his effort to control those who love him, he seeks to be a kind of god.

In his fallen state, however, Clamence feels an almost paranoiac need for friends. He experiences a desperate solitude which his suave manner cannot obscure: "But don't think for a minute that your friends will telephone you every evening, as they ought to, in order to find out if this doesn't happen to be the evening when you are deciding to commit suicide" (p. 33). When faced with the ultimate horror of his life, Clamence, like Roquentin, is driven to a desire for the very companions he once disdained as unworthy of him.

The man who listens to the hero's confession is a visitor from Paris, a representative of the society Clamence had once looked down upon. The hero would never have invited such a man to join him at "the soaring peaks" of his early life, but he now exercises all his powers to lure him into his underground hell. He acts as a sort of guide through Amsterdam's dead-smelling canals (which he compares to the rivers of hell), fog, and the motionless, eerie Zuider Zee. As a successful lawyer, Clamence had been aloof, choosing words carefully; in the Amsterdam bar, he is bold in introducing himself to a stranger, gregarious in telling his anecdotes. Superficially, he is typical of many lonely men in lonely bars, telling their troubles; but the words are still carefully selected to draw his companion closer to him. Among the several themes expressed by these mannerisms, that of isolation is a subtly stated but important one.

When Dostoevsky rejected rationalism and determinism and reaffirmed the value of freedom for the modern world, he opened the way to extensive considerations of that enduring philosophical problem. The confessional novels which follow him are particularly concerned. Richard B. Sewall states the new condition which is established by the Underground Man and which provides the moral framework for the Karamazov world: "The only hope for man in his new state of spiritual anarchy is to follow out his nature wherever it leads; he must test his new freedom to the very limit."[11] The hero of *The Immoralist* echoes this idea: "To know how to free oneself is nothing; the arduous thing is to know what to do with one's freedom" (p. 7).

11. Sewall, *The Vision of Tragedy,* p. 110.

In the early stages of his sickness, Michel drifts helplessly, depending on Marceline's strength and sinking in his own self-pity. Then the strange episode in the garden at Biskra brings him "the tragic realization of my life" and a resolution to conquer his infirmity. He begins to develop his terrible Nietzschean creed of power and strength and seizes on every example of daring action—from the young thief Moktir to the most complete Nietzschean "superman," Menalque.

The "terrible imbalance" of internal and external forces remains, however, and turns his affirmations of freedom into a cruel paradox. Although he revels in the risks of others, Michel himself is incapable of such action. When he boldly dismisses two tenant farmers, he proves unable to work their farms successfully and begins the destruction of his estate. His poaching ends in a debacle which leaves him inferior to the corrupt boys as well as to Charles, the righteous and stuffy young man. As his outward efforts flounder, the creed which grips his mind grows increasingly turbulent and obsessive, culminating in the destruction of Marceline. This conflict of desire with inability to act also parallels the psychological drama of latent drives and suppression which is always just beneath the surface of Michel's actions.

Another aspect of the paradoxical freedom of *The Immoralist* is expressed shortly after Michel's dramatic resolution at Biskra: "I did not think all this at the time, and my description gives a false idea of me. In reality, I did not think at all; I never questioned myself; a happy fatalism guided me" (p. 44). It soon becomes apparent that his absolute faith in strength and his own power—which in itself seems to affirm his freedom—is actually depriving him of any true freedom to think clearly and control his actions. Later, during his compulsive travels, he acknowledges the damage he is doing to Marceline's frail health, but wonders, "Had I the power to choose what I should determine—to decide what I should desire?" (p. 132) And on still another journey, he cries, "Will nothing make me stop?" Michel has answered his own initial question of what to do with one's free-dom; he has thrown it away.

Antoine Roquentin speaks frequently of his freedom in the early pages of *Nausea*. Of the "monotonous sorrow" of Lucie the charwoman, he says, "She is bound" (p. 21). Roquentin himself, by the nature of his separation from people like Lucie or the café patrons, considers himself free. Sartre has elsewhere equated the inward-directed consciousness with freedom: "For a conscious-ness to be able to imagine it must be able to escape from the world by its very nature, it must be able by its own efforts to withdraw from the world. In a word it must be free."[12] For Sartre, however, freedom is a state which allows man to make choices, and those choices inevitably leave him responsible for them. "I never en-counter anything but my responsibility," he writes in *Being and Nothingness*.[13] Roquentin shares this feeling: "I staggered under the weight of my responsibility" (p. 87). Frequently, this pressing responsibility obscures freedom itself, leaving the hero in a des-pairing and painful state of solitude. At the end of one meditation on his loneliness, Roquentin says ruefully, "All I wanted was to be free" (p. 91).

Ultimately, however, the freedom which Roquentin claims is superficial. He is not bound by women or a group of companions; he can travel where he wishes, work when he pleases. But all these apparent liberties prove hollow. He is plagued by thoughts of Anny; his proud aloofness turns to painful isolation; he remains immobile in the oppressive Bouville atmosphere he dislikes; and he finds himself unable to write his book. This suppression of his real freedom is illustrated early, when he tells of his love of picking up filthy scraps of paper from gutters—clearly an act free

12. Sartre makes this statement in *The Psychology of the Imagination;* it is cited in Fernando Molina's *Existentialism as Philosophy* (Englewood Cliffs, N.J., Spectrum, 1962), p. 84.

13. Sartre, *Being and Nothingness,* trans. Hazel Barnes (New York, Philosophical Library, 1956), p. 556.

of conventional rules of behavior. When he prepares to enjoy this strange habit in Bouville, he fails:

> I bent down, already rejoicing at the touch of this pulp, fresh and tender, which I should roll in my fingers into greyish balls . . . I was unable.
>
> I stayed bent down for a second, I read "Dictation: The White Owl," then I straightened up, empty-handed. I am no longer free, I can no longer do what I will. (p. 19)

From this point onward, in spite of his haughty protestations of separation from the common citizens of Bouville, Roquentin is not truly independent or free. Only when he has stripped himself of all the ties which hold him, culminating in his decision to leave Bouville, can he again claim real freedom. Even then, it is composed only of the direct confrontation with his own existence —his "responsibility." Such a freedom, gained only through intense suffering, proves as problematical as its very absence had seemed before:

> I am free: there is absolutely no more reason for living, all the ones I have tried have given way and I can't imagine any more of them. I am still fairly young, I still have enough strength to start again. But do I have to start again? How much, in the strongest of my terrors, my disgusts, I had counted on Anny to save me I realized only now. My past is dead. The Marquis de Rollebon is dead, Anny came back only to take all hope away. I am alone in this white, garden-rimmed street. Alone and free. But this freedom is rather like death. (p. 209)

Roquentin has achieved a perception, one of the goals of the confessional hero. But it is a very negative perception, a vision of past mistakes, holding only a faint glimmer of hope for the future, for "starting again." In this dark, deathlike freedom, however, the hero does achieve something approaching the state of the jazz record which does hold a positive hope for him: a state which "has nothing superfluous . . . It *is*" (p. 233).

Any discussion of the concept of freedom in *Nausea* must remain inadequate without a fuller treatment of Sartre's philosophy. The above ideas, however, offer several significant insights into the role of freedom in the confessional novel. Freedom is necessary for man, offering him his only unclouded perception of himself; yet it is also the starting point of all his wrong choices, his crucial errors and sins. In *The Immoralist,* freedom opens "the possibilities of life" to Michel; but in his quest for them, he loses freedom itself. For Antoine Roquentin, freedom holds meaning and perception; but these values are inextricably bound to oppressive responsibilities, to the "horror of existence," and to the specter of death. In these equivocal and often paradoxical ways, freedom demands the concern of the sincere confessional hero.

In *The Fall,* Camus carries the idea of freedom one step further; even in the insincere hero, it must be present. Like all crucial themes in the novel, freedom must be considered on two levels, that of the hero's confession and that of the actual truth which rests just beyond the words in the realm of mocking laughter.

"I have never been really able to believe that human affairs were serious matters," Clamence proclaims (p. 86). In this playful guise, he calls himself "an enlightened advocate of slavery" and engages in what seem to be a few colorful anecdotes and satiric observations. He points out the two Negro heads which once served as the shop sign of an old slave dealer, then ridicules modern hypocrisy, which would frown on such a display: "Slavery?—certainly not, we are against it! That we should be forced to establish it at home or in our factories—well, that's natural; but boasting about it, that's the limit!" (p. 44) As with most of his ideas, this one is broached cautiously, apparently only half-seriously; then it reappears several times in references to servants or criminal cases. Finally it bursts into full life in one of the most shocking moments of Clamence's confession. The "judge–penitent," obsessed and tortured by the guilt he sees in himself and others, decides that freedom is not worth the price men pay for it. Having been at various times a demonic parody of the penitent, the judge, and the pope, Clamence combines all three into a resurrection of the Grand Inquisitor:

> I deny the good intention. . . . In philosophy as in politics, I am for any theory that refuses to grant man innocence and for any practice that treats him as guilty. . . . Without slavery, as a matter of fact, there is no definitive solution. . . . At the end all freedom is a court sentence; that's why freedom is too heavy to bear, especially when you're down with a fever, or are distressed, or love nobody. (pp. 132–33)

This is at once a bold, cruel vision and an admission of defeat. A self-proclaimed "empty prophet for shabby times," Clamence evokes the most terrible voice of his generation, that of Hitler, as well as the voice which Dostoevsky felt compelled to negate. At the same time, he turns from the crucial and unresolved problems of freedom which were bequeathed to him by Gide and Sartre —indeed, by the entire modern era—and seeks a world in which "everything should become simple." He has abandoned the honesty required of the true confessional hero.

In a typical use of his brilliant irony, Camus begins to inject the reality of Clamence's position at the end of the proud speech quoted above. The original Grand Inquisitor had his grand vision blurred by a silent kiss. Clamence's modern version of that code collapses along with the crumbling self-control of its creator. At its climax, Clamence reaches the peak of pride which earlier in life had led him to compare himself to a god. He revels in the thought of "power and the whip," imposing order arbitrarily on all those below him. Then he suddenly lapses into his first sincere personal reference since he began to describe his ideas: "But on the bridges of Paris I, too, learned that I was afraid of freedom" (p. 136). This leads to his admission of the deceitful basis for his entire speech to his listener. Although he calls this method of confession a "solution" for his guilt, Clamence is increasingly unable to hide the fact that it has actually solved nothing. Even his physical discomfort reflects his hopeless position, from which there can be no relief: "Open the window a little, please; it's frightfully hot. Not too much, for I am cold also" (p. 137). Moments later, he reveals that his torture remains with him—"I occasionally hear a distant laugh." These relatively subtle admissions convey a growing feeling which finally bursts into vivid relief in the hero's frenzied claim to happiness. In his desperate and patently false cry, Clamence reveals the depth of his long-suppressed suffering and abandons the demeanor which has made his false confession possible. Alongside his pitiful plea for justification ("I won't let you think I'm not happy!"), his merciless vision of an enslaved world loses much of its portent.

Although he repudiates his hero's idea of a world without freedom—as he does all such "simple solutions" for man's condition—Camus does acknowledge the possibility that an individual might lose his own freedom; Jean-Baptiste Clamence has done so. The terrible confinement which guilt imposes upon Clamence is expressed in the striking image of the "little-ease." In this mental equivalent of a medieval torture cell, man is denied the space to extend himself to his full length; living in a series of cramped and deforming diagonal positions, he is not free even to be himself. It is this picture of man enslaved by his own guilt, rather than by any universal order, which Camus accepts as one possible consequence of the disintegrating self.

The recurrent themes of isolation and lost freedom in the confessional heroes of Gide, Sartre, and Camus lead to a profound feeling of impotence—a loss of the power not only to communicate with others and find a "niche" in the world, but also to perform any meaningful action at all. Hence, for the hero of *The Immoralist,* life becomes an unthinking and uncontrolled plunge toward destruction; in *Nausea* and *The Fall,* the loss of power is expressed in immobility, and the heroes are rendered increasingly helpless by their respective states of "the Nausea" and the "little-ease."

The problem of powerlessness introduces one characteristic which distinguishes the special vision of disintegration in these three novels from many of the other treatments of this theme in modern literature. For the confessional heroes of Gide, Sartre, and Camus, disintegration is not a static condition of life. All have known freedom and power and suffer from the loss of these values, rather than from a total absence of such values throughout their lives. Even their most degrading and painful moments cannot completely obscure the "soaring heights" of past experience.

This quality separates these heroes from one conception of modern man's disintegration which would deny even past power. T. S. Eliot's "Gerontion," for example, is "an old man in a dry month," who looks back at his past and sees only a void:

> I was neither at the hot gates
> Nor fought in the warm rain
> Now knee deep in the salt marsh, heaving a cutlass[14]

These three French novelists are closer to the idea expressed by Hart Crane in the "Van Winkle" poem from *The Bridge*—that even at the most mundane and meaningless level, modern man can find some value in the past:

> You walked with Pizarro in a copybook,
> And Cortez rode up, reigning tightly in—
> Firmly as coffee grips the taste,—and away!
>
> There was Priscilla's cheek close to the wind,
> And Captain Smith, all beard and certainty,
> And Rip Van Winkle bowing by the way,—
> "Is this Sleepy Hollow, friend—?" And he—

14. T. S. Eliot, "Gerontion," in *The Complete Poems and Plays, 1909–1950* (New York, Harcourt, Brace and World, 1962), p. 21.

> And Rip forgot the office hours,
> and he forgot the pay;
> Van Winkle sweeps a tenement
> way down on Avenue A,—
>
> The grind-organ says . . . Remember, remember[15]

As long as "Cortez and Pizarro" or Clamence's "lofty places" or Roquentin's "adventures" remain in man's past, even the bleakest vision of disintegration cannot be empty or static; it becomes instead a downward movement, a grim reenactment of man's fall.

The confessional hero who finds himself engaged in such a plunge is compelled to consider what lies at the end of his fall; among the possibilities, there is always death. The problem of death has already been connected with aspects of freedom and isolation, but it is pervasive enough in these three novels to require further consideration.

In *The Immoralist,* the hero engages in little philosophical speculation on death. It is seen primarily as a tremendous force at one pole of the code of absolutes which Michel develops. "Look not too long in the face of fire, O man!" warns Ishmael in *Moby Dick.*[16] Yet Melville forces his narrator to look on the "fire" of Ahab's tragedy until it is finally consummated, and Ishmael is compelled to abandon his former carefree attitude and reconstruct the grim tale. Similarly, Gide's hero is driven by illness to a direct confrontation with death. True to the warning of Ishmael, the fiery specter of death changes Michel's entire life,

15. Hart Crane, *The Bridge,* in *The Complete Poems of Hart Crane,* (Garden City, N.Y., Doubleday Anchor, 1958), p. 13.

16. Herman Melville, *Moby Dick* (New York, Dell, 1959), p. 461. In *The Vision of Tragedy,* Sewall emphasizes Ishmael's early optimism, "seemingly invulnerable to any Jovian thunderclap," and suggests that Ishmael represents the "untragic American audience" which Melville slowly leads toward tragic truth. Michel, the young intellectual so *dégagé* that he calmly marries a near-stranger, is slowly led to his own "fire" by sickness (and by the author), although his reaction to it is self-destructive rather than tragic.

stripping him of what Sartre would have called his "shields against the fact of existence" and initiating the formulation of a new creed:

> After that touch from the wing of Death, what seemed important is so no longer; other things become so which had at first seemed unimportant, or which one did not even know existed. The miscellaneous mass of acquired knowledge of every kind that has overlain the mind gets peeled off in places like a mask of paint, exposing the bare skin—the very flesh of the authentic creature that had lain beneath it. (p. 43)

This is one of the richest and most ironic passages in *The Immoralist,* and it indicates the self-delusion and futility inherent in Michel's blind flight from death. The hero thinks he understands the meaning of his life; however, his admission that his "mask" has peeled off only "in places" foreshadows the danger of building an absolute code on such partial evidence. Sections of the mask cling to Michel in a mockery of the "authentic creature" he claims to have discovered within himself. Ironically, he proceeds through three years of life and his entire confession before he acknowledges, in the final lines of the novel, the internal "creature" which really possesses him. After Marceline's death, he becomes close to a young boy and his older sister, a prostitute; at the boy's insistence, he gives up his relations with the girl. In this affair, for the first time, he faces his inner drives: "Every time I meet her, she laughs and declares that I prefer the boy to her. She makes out that it is he who keeps me here. Perhaps she is not altogether wrong" (p. 147). The illusion created by Michel's first look at death has finally been clarified, but it is too late to save Marceline's life or his own disintegrated spirit.

Shortly after his crucial experience on the Paris bridge, the hero of *The Fall* says, "Then it was that the thought of death burst into my daily life" (p. 89). This is characteristic of the view of death in Camus and Sartre; as soon as the hero becomes aware of his disintegration or fall, he is preoccupied with the thought of the death which awaits him. In *Being and Nothingness,* Sartre describes death as "the simultaneous disappearance of the for-itself and of the world, of the subjective and the objective, of the significant and of all meanings."[17] The overwhelming finality of these words is modulated only by the fact that one lives on in the memory of others. While Sartre the philosopher may find solace in this qualification, however, his hero in *Nausea* cannot. He has isolated himself from others, and his own experience with the Marquis de Rollebon has denied the possibility of a living, enduring past. Since he has resolved to find meaning only in his present self, Roquentin finds death "the disappearance of all meanings," a terrifying specter.

It is significant that Roquentin's obsession with death begins moments after his realization of "the weight of my responsibility." In the café, he watches the powerful, overbearing Doctor Roge and finds a strange satisfaction in the man's mortality:

> The truth stares me in the face: this man is going to die soon.
> . . . The doctor would like to believe, he would like to hide
> out the stark reality; that he is alone, without gain, without
> a past, with an intelligence which is clouded, a body which
> is disintegrating. . . . That would give him a jolt if he could
> say to himself: "There's someone who *knows* I'm going to
> die!" (pp. 96–97)

It soon becomes clear, however, that these contemptuous words also describe the hero himself. Brombert notes "the extent to which the Sartrean intellectual needs the other in order to feel the contempt for himself he *wants* to feel."[18] Roquentin's meditations on the mortality of others are a striking indication of this tendency.

When the café manager does not appear the following day, Roquentin cannot free himself of the nagging idea that the man

17. Sartre, *Being and Nothingness,* p. 545.
18. Brombert, p. 190.

may be dead. His attempt to scoff at his own thoughts ("Just the kind of ideas you get on foggy days") fails miserably, and an entire day is dominated by this strange concern. He is subsequently tormented by similar thoughts about de Rollebon, about obscure figures painted in the Bouville gallery, and even about the Autodidact. Gradually, he begins to acknowledge the personal significance of this morbid progression. Before a portrait of one deceased citizen, he thinks, "This painting gave me a last warning: there was still time, I could retrace my steps" (p. 113).

In the dark vision of *Nausea,* however, death is more than a force which goads the hero in his quest for meaning. Roquentin's disillusioning admission that his long-sought freedom "is rather like death" intimates that his philosophical life may face the same inevitable end as his physical existence. In a sense, death *is* a state "with nothing superfluous," like the purified existence Roquentin seeks. As such, it shows the emptiness of the condition Roquentin achieves by merely stripping himself of all social and physical ties. In his one redemptive moment, Roquentin finally perceives the saving quality Sartre presents in *Being and Nothingness*—the possibility of creating something "beyond death," which might simultaneously bring meaning to life before death. He sees this in the Jew and the Negress who created the jazz record he loves:

> They are a little like dead people for me, a little like the heroes of a novel; they have washed themselves of the sin of existing. Not completely, of course, but as much as any man can. This idea suddenly knocks me over, because I was not even hoping for that any more. (p. 237)

At the end of a life dedicated to cutting himself off from others, the hero thus finds in death a reason to consider other people. When he resolves to write a novel, he thinks in terms which he would have ridiculed at the beginning of his journal:

> There would be people who would read this book and say: "Antoine Roquentin wrote it, a red-headed man who hung

around cafés," and they would think about my life as I
think about the negress's: as something precious and almost
legendary. (p. 238)

The idea of death, the powerful negative theme of much of his
journal, has ultimately led to its only positive hope, the hope that
"I might succeed—in the past, nothing but the past—in accepting
myself."

The idea that, while rejecting all possibility of a life after
death,[19] man can still find perception in death is also important
in Camus' novels. In an essay on *The Stranger,* Sartre illuminates
one view of death which these two authors share:

The absurd man will not commit suicide; he wants to live,
without relinquishing any of his certainty, without a future,
without hope, without illusion, and without resignation
either. He stares at death with passionate attention and this
fascination liberates him.[20]

R. W. B. Lewis clarifies this point when he cites Camus' "tena-
cious confrontation of death as the only way of getting at an
honest and even a positive estimate of life."[21]

Meursault, the hero of *The Stranger,* experiences such a "lib-
eration" on the eve of his execution, when he looks back on his
life and realizes "that I'd been happy, and that I was happy

19. Camus' denial of an afterlife is stated most succinctly in his early
essays, *Noces.* In an essay entitled "Camus the Pagan" (*Yale French
Studies,* No. 25 [Spring 1960], pp. 20–25), Henri Peyre comments on that
denial: " 'I do not choose to believe,' states the worshipper of the wind at
Djemila, in *Noces,* 'that death opens onto another life. To me it is a closed
door.' Those delusions are but an attempt to unburden man of the weight
of his own life. And Camus prefers to carry his burden himself."
20. Sartre, "An Explication of *The Stranger"* (1947), rep. in Brée, ed.,
Camus: A Collection of Critical Essays (Englewood Cliffs, N.J., Spectrum
[Twentieth Century Views Series], 1962), p. 110.
21. R. W. B. Lewis, *The Picaresque Saint* (Philadelphia, J. B. Lippincott, 1958), p. 73.

still."[22] The hero of *The Fall,* however, is denied such a confrontation with death and ultimate perception, due to the very nature
of his false confession. He looks wistfully at death as another
"simple solution," an end to the doubts which plague his existence: "In order to cease being a doubtful case, one has to cease
being, that's all" (p. 75). At the same time, he lacks the courage
to face death. Thus, for Clamence, death becomes both a compulsive force in his life and an empty hope for relief from that life.
For one brief interval, he sees it as Camus himself did, as an
impetus to a real perception of one's existence:

> I was tormented by the thought that I might not have time
> to accomplish my task. What task? I had no idea. Frankly,
> was what I was doing worth continuing? But that was not
> quite it. A ridiculous fear pursued me, in fact: one could not
> die without having confessed all one's lies. (pp. 89–90)

But the very fact that he considers this idea "ridiculous" negates
its potential value, and Clamence condemns himself to darkness
with his boast that "I pulled myself together, of course." He proceeds to compound his lies, and death ceases to be a force and
becomes only a vague notion of escape. This aspect of the hero's
view is articulated most clearly in his cry of hopelessness: "Ah,
who would have believed that crime consists less in making others
die than in not dying oneself!" (p. 113)

Like his vision of an enslaved world, Clamence's idea of death
is finally destroyed. He conjures up an image of his own death,
which is a parody not only of Christ and John the Baptist, but also
of the positive aspects of death which Sartre and Camus affirm:

> I would be decapitated, for instance, and I'd have no more
> fear of death; I'd be saved. Above the gathered crowd, you

22. Camus, *The Stranger,* trans. Stuart Gilbert (New York, Vintage,
1954), p. 154.

> would hold up my still warm head, so that they could recognize themselves in it and I could again dominate—an exemplar. All would be consummated; I should have brought to a close, unseen and unknown, my career as a false prophet crying in the wilderness and refusing to come forth. (pp. 146–47)

In such a death, the hero would clearly not be "saved" and would leave nothing which might live on in the manner of Roquentin's projected novel. But the brutal irony of this passage lies not only in Clamence's failure to achieve these positive effects; he has also returned to the pride and desire to be an "exemplar" which led to his initial fall. This vision of death gives tremendous power to his final admission that he would never want "a second chance" to save the girl on the bridge and to the bleak comfort he takes in the fact that "It's too late now. It will always be too late. Fortunately!" (p. 147)

Having examined some major themes in *The Immoralist, Nausea,* and *The Fall,* we can begin to establish the significance of these novels within the confessional genre. In structure, the confessional novels of Gide and Camus are distinct from those of Sartre; the former bear more resemblance to their Dostoevskian forerunner, *Notes from the Underground,* while Sartre's use of the diary form recalls earlier and more traditional forms of confession. Gide and Camus both called their short novels *récits,* or tales, a name which carries wider implications than its apparent declaration of modesty of intention. Albert Guerard says that Gide saw his *récits* "as concentrated critical studies of a single character or a single problem."[23] They also implied a dissociation of the author from his character, emphasizing an "ironic detachment from the scene."[24] Rachel Bespaloff adds a final important

23. Guerard, p. 94.
24. Brée and Guiton, p. 231.

characteristic when she notes, in an essay on Camus, "The *récit*, by its very nature, supposes a narrator who arranges past events according to the meaning he confers on them."[25]

The *récit* is a traditional form of French literature,[26] but it is clear that the traits cited above also guided the creator of *Notes from the Underground*. Gide and Camus have combined these two sources to produce a form which is more refined and well-ordered than Dostoevsky's, but which maintains his psychological penetration and much of the urgency of the Underground Man's confession. It is this form, rather than the chronological diary of *Nausea*, which typifies the modern confessional consciousness and its attempt to impose meaningful order on the chaotic events of one's life.

On the other hand, it is Sartre who presents to the confessional novel the most significant French contribution in imagery. Gide and Camus employ images which complement the stories of their heroes. Michel pursues self-discovery and the "possibilities of life" in a vast open space. The momentousness of certain events is emphasized by "the nocturnal shadows in the little courtyard at Biskra" or the "deep transparent waters where, as far as the eye could reach, nothing could be seen but love" (p. 74). Michel's reborn sensuality is constantly emphasized by images of the hot sun or cold rain. In *The Fall,* Camus surrounds his hero with the imagery of the underground, as exemplified in the "little-ease" and the parallels between Amsterdam and hell. The effectiveness of these images is central to the artistic success of the novels, but the images remain in the tradition of all literary imagery. It is Sartre who takes a bold step toward developing original images

25. Rachel Bespaloff, "The World of the Man Condemned to Death," rep. in Brée, ed., p. 92.
26. Guerard discusses the tradition of the *récit,* citing Constant's *Adolphe* as one example which Gide may have followed. Guerard emphasizes the way in which Gide "revived and revitalized" the form, making it "something more than a confession or problem novel, something more than a case study" (*André Gide,* p. 201).

and idioms which are particularly suited to the portrayal of the intellectual hero.

Such an original idiom is necessary if the intense philosophical struggles within the hero are to acquire dramatic import. Brombert cites Sartre's most conspicuous success in this regard:

> The very hum of his brain suggests, hallucinatingly, the drama of thought that makes [Roquentin] both a hero and a victim:
> "I exist. I think that I exist . . . I do not want to think . . . I think that I do not want to think. I must not think that I don't want to think. For that too is a thought. Won't there ever be an end?"

Or again:

> "I am, I exist, I think therefore I am; I am because I think; why do I think? I no longer want to think; I am because I think that I do not want to be; I think that I . . . because . . . pouah!"[27]

The hallucinatory nature of Roquentin's words extends beyond these intensely cerebral passages into a weird and haunting series of images. Sunday morning in Bouville is seen as an inverted funeral procession, in which the citizens take on the aspect of death and solid objects seem to move in preparation for their coming:

> Between the interminable walls of factories, long black processions have started walking, they are slowly advancing toward the center of town. To receive them, the streets have taken on the look they have when disturbance is expected, all the stores . . . have lowered their iron shutters. Soon, silently, these black columns are going to invade the death-shamming streets. (p. 59)

27. Brombert, p. 182.

Similarly, Roquentin imagines the staid, rigidly ordered library being visited by an eerie presence:

> Saint Denis himself could come in carrying his head in his hands and he would still have to enter on the right, walk between the shelves devoted to French Literature and the table reserved for women readers. And if he doesn't touch the ground, if he floats ten inches above the floor, his bleeding neck will be just as the level of the third shelf of books. (pp. 105–06)

The conclusion of this passage—a resigned observation that the shelves "serve at least to fix the limits of probability"—elucidates the function of all such imagery in *Nausea*. It is designed to portray a mind gone beyond conventional limits, a mind which cannot be comprehended in the context of objective reality, but is so unique that only its own strange creations can properly reflect it.

Gide, Sartre, and Camus use another technique which is characteristic of the confessional novel—the role of the double. Menalque accelerates Michel's growing devotion to daring and strength; the Autodidact reflects Roquentin's lowest opinions of himself as an intellectual; Clamence's listener represents his past life in Paris. The aesthetic and psychological ramifications of this technique were discussed in relation to Dostoevsky, and it suffices here merely to note the continued use of the double in these novels as one of the unifying traits of the confessional genre.

The most important French contribution to the conception of the hero in the confessional novel is the development of the intellectual narrator, which has already been treated at some length. In addition, these three novels continue to examine the traits of the hero which are most important to the confession, centering on the problem of honesty. Gide is most demanding in this regard. The hero of *The Immoralist* asks, "What use can this story be to me if it ceases to be truthful?" (p. 141) In *Strait Is the*

Gate, the young narrator pledges his sincerity in the very first paragraph, again emphasizing the important fact that this honesty is not based on any moral rule but is actually *necessary* if the hero is to maintain any hope of perception through his confession:

> I shall set down my recollections quite simply, and if in places they are ragged I shall have recourse to no invention and neither patch nor connect them; any effort I might make to dress them up would take away the last pleasure I hope to get in telling them.[28]

The hero of *Nausea* does not embark on his confession consciously, so his affirmation of the need for honesty develops more gradually, to be fully articulated only in his determination to "rid the moments of their fat" and examine them (and himself) in stark, direct terms. Yet his concern with sincerity is apparent from the start; after only a few pages of his journal, he chides himself, "I have just filled up ten pages and I haven't told the truth—at least, not the whole truth" (p. 18). From that point onward, honesty is a dominant, if subtly stated, trait of his confession.

Camus is more preoccupied with the problem of honesty in *The Fall* than either of his predecessors. In his completely dishonest narrator, he creates the anti-hero of the confessional genre, a man who personifies the ₋egative aspects of the true confessional hero. The fate of Jean-Baptiste Clamence is an unequivocal statement of Camus' own view on the need for sincerity, but the fact that Clamence could exist at all calls the values of the confessional novel into question; the answer to this question, if there is an answer, demands a fuller discussion of *The Fall,* which can be found at the conclusion of this chapter.

Finally, there is the question of how these authors treat the problem of purgation or perception which is crucial to the mean-

28. Gide, *Strait Is the Gate,* trans. Dorothy Bussy (New York, Vintage, 1959), pp. 77–78.

ing of any confessional novel. The answer reemphasizes the predominant theme of all three novels—disintegration. After unraveling their lives and suffering again for their sins, the heroes are left with only a glimmer of the "good" they sought in their confessions. Perception is, at best, vague and partial, less substantial than even the most fleeting visions of Dostoevsky's heroes.

Nausea presents the most significant perception that is achieved in these three novels. It occurs when Roquentin hears the jazz recording of "Some of These Days" and sees in it something outside the destructive realm of existence, something offering a hope for meaning. In his appreciation of the way in which the creators of this record have been "saved," Roquentin resolves to seek a similar salvation by writing a novel. On this note, his journal ends.

This perception, however, is a very limited one. It brings the hero an understanding of the meaning of existence but does not give order to his earlier life; in fact, it only emphasizes the shapelessness of that life. By its very nature, this perception must also be finite and fleeting. Even as he listens to the record, Roquentin realizes that he will not be able to hold on to its meaning: "I'm hearing it for the last time: it is very old, even too old for the provinces; I will look for it in vain in Paris" (p. 232).

In a sense, the question of whether Roquentin will ever really write his novel is as irrelevant to the meaning of *Nausea* as the promise of a "new life" for Raskolnikov is to *Crime and Punishment*. Even if one accepts its relevance, however, there remains serious doubt about whether Roquentin will actually perpetuate his moment of resolution in this way. The "editor's note" at the beginning of the novel seems to indicate that the hero was unable to do so. "These notebooks were found among the papers of Antoine Roquentin," states the "editor," intimating that the hero is no longer present. His death seems most unlikely, especially since suicide would be a denial of all his beliefs. It is more probable that mental derangement has removed him from the world. Such an interpretation compounds the theme of disintegration in the novel and simultaneously heightens its impact, as Brée and Guiton suggest:

> Once the reader is aware of this possibility, the intense and anguished tone of Roquentin's journal, his scrupulous analysis of every mental and emotional reaction, reads like a desperate struggle to cope with impending insanity. This interpretation in no way lessens the impact of the novel: If you, my readers, tried consistently to see things as they really are, Roquentin seems to be telling us, you would also become insane.[29]

In this light, Roquentin's perception becomes a last glimpse of stability in a crumbling consciousness, a perception which can ultimately tell the hero only what he has missed and cannot lead him to new positive values.

The idea that the hero might write a novel in the future leads to an additional possibility: Has Roquentin achieved order in his chaotic existence through the production of his journal itself? As Brée and Guiton rightly point out, "Sartre, unlike Proust, does not imply that his own novel is the very novel his narrator will eventually write."[30] But, although it is not the novel Roquentin plans to write, *Nausea* is the novel he does write. It expresses all the spontaneity and shapelessness of his actual struggle with existence in a manner which a well-planned future novel would not and could not duplicate, and it enables Roquentin's life to live on after him. Its existence—and the probable nonexistence of any future novel by the hero—suggests that, for a man so completely enveloped in the experience of his own existence, the only possible form of expression is the empassioned, spontaneous journal —the confessional novel.

At the conclusion of *The Immoralist,* the hero finally perceives the sources of his guilt. He acknowledges the failure of the creed

29. Brée and Guiton, p. 208.
30. Ibid., pp. 207–08.

by which he has lived, and, in the final lines, he faces his long-suppressed homosexual drives. Michel's is a futile and empty perception, however, occurring too late to save him and remaining too slight to purge him of his guilt. It is a perception without hope, looking backward at his fall but not forward toward regeneration. Its focus on the past only accentuates the total lack of self-perception which has accelerated the hero's doom. He could never see the flaws in his creed while it was leading him away from Marceline into a blind quest for all signs of health, daring, and sensual experience. Even when he naïvely allowed the boys to make a fool of him in the poaching incident and admitted that "I should never know anything about creatures like them" (p. 115), he always failed to see the urgent need for the perception which might have saved him. These frequent illustrations of Michel's imperception heighten the irony and futility of the bitter awareness which he finally does achieve.

At the end of Michel's tale, the reader is left with the same uneasy sensation as the three listeners. There is a vague feeling that, while avoiding commitment himself, Michel has involved others in his confession. This idea is not articulated as in *Notes from the Underground,* but it remains as the only glimmer of justification in Michel's confession. He has perceived his own mistakes but, until this final hint, has been unable to progress from this raw perception to the possibility of purgation. In the introductory letter written by one of Michel's comforters, the strange atmosphere around Michel's confession is described: "The air here fills one with a kind of vague excitement and induces a state as far removed from cheerfulness as it is from sorrow; perhaps it is happiness" (p. 4). One wonders if this electric feeling signifies the coming of grace, the sensation of hope. But one can only wonder, for the hero remains in the dark condition of Job before he was granted perception. He at last sees the futility of his absolute code and the reality of his inner nature, but no new possibilities arise on which he might build a hope for redemption.

Gide creates a more vivid final image of disintegration in the brutally destructive ending to "Alissa's Journal" in *Strait Is the Gate*. Unlike Michel, who is gradually betrayed by his absolute creed, Alissa gives up her own absolute belief in religion in a sudden and convulsive reflex of despair. After her long series of mystical meditations and prayers, Alissa's dramatic realization that she has deceived herself is expressed in terms of the sexual life from which she has fled: "O jealous God, who hast despoiled me, take Thou possession of my heart. All warmth henceforth has forsaken it."[31] In her last entry in the diary before her death, she directly identifies "the sudden and disenchanting *illumination* of my life . . . I should like to die now, quickly, before again realizing that I am alone" (p. 144). This unflinching negation emphasizes the fact that Gide promises no purgation or redemption to his confessional characters. They achieve a bitter perception of their errors, but their suffering continues.

Perception is inevitably and unequivocally denied to Camus' false confessional hero in *The Fall*. The only comforting vision at the end of the novel is offered to the reader, as he sees to his relief that the terrifying elements of Clamence's world are merely the constructions of a sick and deceitful mind. Yet this revelation is ambiguous in itself; the honest reader tends to feel that he cannot really discard Clamence's disturbing accusations. The final decay of Clamence's "play-actor" pose cannot negate the possibility of truth in his vision of a guilt-ridden world. The same mocking laugh which denies purgation to the hero also haunts the peace of any modern man who considers himself immune to the elaborate trap of *The Fall*. Once the superficial forms of perception have been denied to both the hero and his listeners, we can concern ourselves with the true vision of Camus' novel. This vision can be found only by a painstaking effort to distinguish truth from falsehood, reality from satire, and thus to assess Camus' crucial place in confessional literature.

31. Gide, *Strait Is the Gate,* p. 141.

Created within the framework of *Notes from the Underground* and consistently concerned with symbols and ideas from sources in Christian tradition as well as Dostoevsky's work, *The Fall,* it appears, has returned to the origins of confessional consciousness. The traditional influences on the novel, however, are juxtaposed and merged with several distinctly modern themes, whose development has been traced through Gide and Sartre. One such theme is disintegration itself. "Do you know what has become of one of the houses in this city that sheltered Descartes?" asks Clamence. "A lunatic asylum" (p. 116). In such a world of crumbling and chaotic truths, any traditional hope of regeneration must become meaningless. The second crucial idea which Camus inherits from his French predecessors is the possibility of deceit and dishonesty in the confession. This concept, which is foreshadowed in the Underground Man's self-conscious references to his audience, is boldly stated by Sartre. Brombert notes:

> Sartre repeatedly suggests that meditation, deliberation and analysis are perfidious forms of separatism. In *L'Etre et le Neant,* he goes so far as to qualify deliberation as always dishonest (*"la deliberation est* toujours truquee."—p. 527).[32]

Sartre's own confessional novel denies this total rejection of honesty, but the hero of *Nausea* remains deeply conscious of the problem. Camus clearly brought a similar awareness to his own work.

Camus illuminates the intention of *The Fall* in his epigraph, a quotation from Mikhail Lermontov's introduction to his major Russian novel of 1840. By using a nineteenth-century source to describe his desire to create a vision of the modern consciousness, Camus suggests the complex mixture of old and new ideas which takes place throughout the novel. The quotation itself prefigures the haunting accusations which will echo through the world of *The Fall:*

32. Brombert, p. 188.

> Some were dreadfully insulted, and quite seriously, to have held up as a model such an immoral character as *A Hero of Our Time;* others shrewdly noticed that the author had portrayed himself and his acquaintances. . . . *A Hero of Our Time,* gentleman, is in fact a portrait, but not an individual; it is the aggregate of the vices of our whole generation in their fullest expression.

The clash of traditional and modern forces in *The Fall* takes on the aspect of an evasive, partly satiric myth—a re-creation of the Fall of man in a turbulent context which lacks the absolute principles that gave order and meaning to the original event. Clamence falls from a material paradise (a parody of heaven) in which he thinks he is a kind of god into a hell in which he assumes the role of false pope and judge (a parody of Beelzebub). He also becomes a sort of demonic missionary, luring his listener into his own hell. One of several sets of images which illustrate this aspect of his life is the progression of scene changes. Clamence gradually leads his victim out of the relative security of the bar, around the circuitous canals of Amsterdam (the rivers of hell), and onto the Zuider Zee, where the shores become "lost in the fog" and man is forced to proceed "without any landmark." Finally, he invites his listener to his small, stuffy room—a parody of the Catholic confessional—and offers him membership in his demonic community: "I shall listen, you may be sure, to your own confession with a great feeling of fraternity" (p. 140).

Alongside this religious framework there exists the heritage of Dostoevsky. The hero's purpose is modeled on the perception achieved by the Underground Man, and whole incidents in his life reemphasize his affinity for that prototypical confessional hero. One striking example recalls the Underground Man's torture at the hands of his servant Apollon; even in his proud paradise before the fall, Clamence is intensely disturbed by a lowly concierge: "I had one, really ill-favored, malice incarnate, a monster of insignificance and rancor, who would have discouraged a Franciscan. I had even given up speaking to him, but by his mere existence he compromised my customary contentedness" (p. 34). The echo of the Grand Inquisitor in Clamence has already been discussed; the hero's breadth is illuminated when he also touches the other pole of Christian thought in Dostoevsky, the union of responsibility and sacrifice in Father Zossima's world: "Who, *cher monsieur,* will sleep on the floor for us? Whether I am capable of it myself? Look, I'd like to be and I shall be. Yes, we shall all be capable of it one day, and that will be salvation" (p. 32).

This early concern with salvation evolves into Clamence's conception of himself as a "judge–penitent"—another derivation from Dostoevsky. Camus found this idea in Dostoevsky's *Diary of a Writer* and quoted it in *The Myth of Sisyphus* as a possible argument for "logical suicide":

> "Since, finally, in this connection, I assume both the role of the plaintiff and that of the defendant, of the accused and of the judge, and since I consider this comedy perpetrated by nature altogether stupid, and since I even deem it humiliating for me to deign to play it. . . . In my indisputable capacity of plaintiff and defendant, of judge and accused, I condemn that nature which, with such impudent nerve, brought me into being in order to suffer—I condemn it to be annihilated with me."[33]

The relevance of this argument to the problem of suicide is discussed in *The Myth of Sisyphus,* but the image of the judge–penitent is retained, to be reexamined in *The Fall.*

The world of Jean-Baptiste Clamence is almost by definition a refutation of the possibility of a modern judge–penitent, a hero who will suffer for the sins of man and then pass judgment on his

33. Camus, *The Myth of Sisyphus,* trans. Justin O'Brien (New York, Vintage, 1959), pp. 77–78.

fellowmen. Clearly, the only such figure is Christ, and Christ cannot exist in the enslaved hell of Clamence's vision. Hence, the hero's role as judge–penitent becomes another aspect of the irony of *The Fall,* a parody of Christ which offers only suffering and condemnation to man.

This disturbing series of parodies of revered principles of order creates the overall mood of disintegration which rests at the center of the novel. As one value after another is exposed as illusory or irrelevant, Camus forces us to grasp at any hint of true meaning. The delineation between parody and reality is so blurred that one can never be fully confident that Clamence's accusations do not hold some truth. It is this vague quality which has led some critics to see in *The Fall* "a realization of sin and unworthiness . . . the dark night before the coming of grace"[34] or to equate Clamence's fate with the "fortunate fall" of Christian tradition, making possible a future enrichment and humanization.[35] Such hopeful views seem to deemphasize Camus' satire to too great an extent. On the other hand, Henri Peyre sees the novel as an almost total satire, denying all possibilities for meaningful confession:

> The hero of *The Fall* is an embittered, sarcastic nihilist, a garrulous talker merging his own guilt in the guilt which he instills in all those whom he forces to listen to him. If anything, that baffling tale should be read as a satire of the self-

34. Bernard C. Murchland, C.S.C., offers this interpretation. He sees Camus at the end of "a pilgrimage through absurdity to a high sense of purpose," joining ranks with "the Mauriac-Greene tradition." His essay, "The Dark Night Before the Coming of Grace," first published in *Catholic World* (January 1959), is reprinted in Brée, ed., pp. 59–64.

35. R. W. B. Lewis sees Clamence's fate as a "fortunate fall" (p. 107), emphasizing that he means a "humanistic equivalent of the religious idea," in which the fall from virtue can "educate, enrich and humanize the hero." These are interesting possibilities for Clamence, but I would dispute Lewis' statement that Clamence "is a much fuller human being" after the fall. In the final scene he is defeated and disintegrated to a point at which he seems less "human" than he had been even in his vainest moments in Paris.

indictment practiced by Christians and atheistic Existentialists alike.[36]

To distill a coherent meaning from this controversial novel, it is necessary to turn away from the seemingly hopeless effort to divide sincerity from satire and concentrate on the more attainable delineation between the author and his confessional hero. As a hero, Jean-Baptiste Clamence is the end product of the current of disintegration which pervades the confessional novels of Gide and Sartre. He has lost the one redeeming quality which makes confession possible for even the most tormented sinner—honesty. Since he is determined to use his confession in order to hide his own sin and focus on those of others, he can find no meaning in it, and, in fact, distorts the traditional confessional forms to the extent that they seem to lose all relevance to the modern world. He is, in his own phrase, "an empty prophet"—a dead end in the development of the confessional hero.

The novel as a whole, however, need not be seen in terms of such total negation. Its central ambiguity, the problem of distinguishing truth from satire, actually provides an impetus toward a renewed confessional tradition, for even after the fate of the hero is sealed, his haunting accusations remain. Although he has failed to draw the reader completely into his community of guilt, Clamence has succeeded in throwing the accepted principles of life into confusion. All his "simple solutions" have been renounced by the author, but they have been replaced only by an acknowledgment of the complexity of the world. The confusion remains.

Sartre said that Camus is "very much at peace within disorder,"[37] but most men cannot share that feeling of peace. *The Fall* leaves us with a profound awareness of the possibility of our own guilt and a pervasive uncertainty about the values of life. At this nadir of disintegration, man is compelled to grope for new

36. Peyre, "Camus the Pagan," p. 23.
37. Sartre, "An Explication of *The Stranger*," p. 116.

values and meanings, to seek the elusive line which separates reality from the mocking laughter of *The Fall*. More than ever before, the urgency of the confessional hero has been transferred to an entire age. Man's desire for order in such an age of uncertainty affirms the enduring relevance of the self-examination inherent in the modern confessional novel.

3. THE SEARCH FOR A RECONSTRUCTED ORDER:

Koestler and Golding

Confronted with the disintegration and uncertainty of the modern condition, man is challenged to find new principles of order and meaning to guide his existence. Nietzsche, the prophet of the age of disintegration portrayed in the confessional novels of Gide, Sartre, and Camus, was strikingly aware of its inherent challenge:

> Why has the advent of nihilism become necessary? Because the values we have had hitherto thus draw their final consequence; because nihilism represents the ultimate logical conclusion of our great values and ideals—because we must

experience nihilism before we can find out what value these "values" really had.—We require, at some time, new values.[1]

One way in which man seeks these new values is through a re-examination of the old ones and of himself; thus, the quest for a reconstructed order leads him to the confessional form. In two modern confessional novels, the heroes examine themselves in relation to wider systems of existence and produce new and important statements on the possibility of order. These works are Arthur Koestler's *Darkness at Noon* (1941) and William Golding's *Free Fall* (1959).

The heroes of these novels approach systems of order in very different ways. Rubashov, the old Communist of *Darkness at Noon,* has served his system for forty years; his confession is an effort to learn what went wrong with it and whether he can find any meaning for life outside it. On the other hand, Sammy Mountjoy, the hero of *Free Fall,* describes a life spent constantly searching for a system. Both heroes finally reach the conclusion that cold, logical formulas for existence cannot solve the problems of our time; truth and meaning, they discover, can be found only in an understanding of the self and its relation to the world.

Koestler and Golding clearly recognize the theme of disintegration which dominates the confessional novels of Gide, Sartre, and Camus, but they approach it with a spirit of hope which is absent in those French novels—a hope that meaning and order can still be constructed upon the chaotic foundations of our time. Even as he admits the failure of the Communist solution, Koestler's hero insists that it must somehow be repaired or replaced:

> There is still a lot to do. The cause of our Party's defectiveness must be found. All our principles were right, but our results were wrong. This is a diseased century. We diagnosed

1. Friedrich Nietzsche, *The Will to Power,* rep. in Kaufmann, ed., *Existentialism from Dostoevsky to Sartre,* p. 110.

this disease and its causes with microscopic exactness, but wherever we applied the healing knife a new sore appeared.[2]

The deep frustration expressed in this statement is tempered by a certain indomitable hope which pervades *Darkness at Noon* and compels the hero onward in his quest for understanding.

The sense of hope in the face of a disintegrating world is more dramatically portrayed in one scene from *Free Fall*. Sammy Mountjoy is writhing in a tiny cell of a Nazi prison camp, terrified by an unknown object at the center of the dark compartment. Gradually, the disintegration of his moral state is translated into brutal physical terms. "My body had many hairs . . . each had its own life. . . . My knees had their automatic fear, too," he says.[3] His loss of control over his own body reaches a painful extreme:

> I let my fingers creep out of my corner. . . . The concrete was changing, was not the same, was smoother.
> Smooth. Wet. Liquid.
> My hand snatched itself back. . . .
> The eye was stung where a flung-back nail
> had grazed the ball, one deep physical
> automatism outsmarted by another. (p. 179)

These sensations drive Sammy toward capitulation, and he finally admits defeat with the Kafkan cry of a subhuman being: "My cry for help was the cry of a rat when the terrier shakes it, a hopeless sound, the raw signature of one savage act. My cry meant no more, was instinctive" (p. 184). This is a portrayal of disintegration as grim as any in Sartre or Camus, but it is followed by a vivid image of hope and regeneration. The unthink-

2. Arthur Koestler, *Darkness at Noon*, trans. Daphne Hardy (New York, Signet, 1961), p. 59. (Henceforth quotations from this novel will be identified by page numbers in parentheses.)
3. William Golding, *Free Fall* (New York, Harbinger, 1962), pp. 177–78. (Henceforth quotations from this novel will be identified by page numbers in parentheses.)

ing, subhuman victim in the cell begins to reason again as he seeks a means of escape:

> The rat struck again from the place away from now into time. It struck with full force backwards into time past, saw with the urgency of present need that time past held only balm for a quieter moment; turned therefore and lunged, uncoiled, struck at the future. (p. 185)

This seems a rather expansive meditation for a desperate and terrified being who is supposed to lack almost all his reasoning powers, but it does serve to emphasize the transformation which Sammy undergoes at the nadir of his disintegration. In his frantic lunge, he says, he "left all living behind. . . . And burst that door." As he leaves the cell, his new commitment to the future strips him of both the comforting self-delusion and the suffering of his past. He is ready for confession: "The eyes of Sammy turned and looked where Halde [his interrogator] had directed them. . . . The eyes of Sammy were turned in on myself with that same stripped and dead objectivity" (p. 190).

It is characteristic of the shifting and elusive temporal sequence of *Free Fall* that the hero has waited until late in his narrative before revealing this episode, the starting point and motivation of his confession. Once the event is presented, however, the redemptive nature of that confession is emphasized. Sammy's account is explicitly religious: "I walked between the huts, a man resurrected . . . I was visited by the flake of fire, miraculous and pentecostal; and fire transmuted me, once and for ever" (pp. 186–88). Throughout his life, Sammy has tried various systems—from Christianity through rationalism and Communism—and found only disappointment and pain. The hopeful vision of the prison camp indicates that, like Rubashov, Sammy has finally realized that the external systems are inadequate and that truth must ultimately be sought in an understanding of the self.

In addition to this movement from abstract to personal systems of value, there are several other affinities between *Darkness at*

Noon and *Free Fall*. Each hero is painfully aware of the uncertain state of his world. Rubashov's reference to this "diseased century" is echoed in Sammy's reaction to the coming of war in Europe: "There was anarchy in the mind where I lived and anarchy in the world at large, two states so similar that one might have produced the other" (p. 132). The heroes' descriptions of the order they seek are also related. Rubashov frequently calls Communism "the equation," and Sammy emphasizes his desire for "a pattern that will include me."

Finally, each of these novels is a kind of religious document. The consistent religious metaphor of *Free Fall* begins with the title itself and includes a series of confrontations with representatives of orthodox religion. Frank Kermode points out several other allusions which confirm Sammy Mountjoy's role as a kind of Everyman: "A central event of his life, as of Dante's, is the recognition of the beauty of a girl called Beatrice. . . . He is subjected by a German officer named Halde to an interrogation modelled on that of Christ in the desert."[4] In *Darkness at Noon,* the hero never directly confronts any formal religion; nevertheless, he frequently uses religious terms to describe his system. Of Lenin and Stalin (not mentioned by name), he says, "He was God the Father, and No. 1 is the Son." He laments that "Revolutionary theory has frozen into a dogmatic cult, with a simplified, easily graspable catechism, and with No. 1 as the high priest celebrating the Mass" (p. 151).

The infusion of a religious fervor into the secular confessions in these novels is central to their overall meaning. It carries the quest of each hero beyond the intellectual effort to find an equation, implying that a meaningful system will offer not merely a cold, logical solution, but a kind of redemption. It also suggests the total commitment which such a system demands of the hero. This idea of commitment helps to account for Rubashov's deep loyalty to Communism in the face of his increasing disillusion-

4. Frank Kermode, "The Novels of William Golding," *International Literary Annual, 3* (1961), 27–28.

ment, and it foreshadows the way in which Sammy Mountjoy sacrifices his freedom in the single-purposed pursuit of his one goal.

The religious themes in these two novels culminate in the remarkably similar visions embraced by the heroes at the climactic moments of their confessions. Each turns away from the "simple solution" of a rigid external system and achieves a heightened perception of the individual self and its relation to the world. Rubashov calls this concept the "oceanic sense," in which "one's personality dissolved as a grain of salt in the sea; but at the same time the infinite sea seemed to be contained in the grain of salt" (p. 213). Sammy's idea is less mystical but quite similar: "The substance was a kind of vital morality, not the relationship of a man to remote posterity or even to a social system, but the relationship of individual man to individual man" (p. 189). It should be emphasized, however, that these redemptive visions are shrouded in ambiguity by the images of disillusionment and guilt which surround them. An understanding of their ultimate significance within the modern confessional genre demands a more detailed consideration of the two novels.

Because of its weighty ideological content, the confession of Nicolas Salmanovitch Rubashov might have been a mere polemical tract, obscuring the true nature of the hero behind his political meditations. Koestler's success in avoiding this pitfall is described by Peter Viereck: "Were it only political history, *Darkness at Noon* would remain narrow and two-dimensional. Its artistic vision is what adds a third dimension of human depth and even . . . a fourth dimension of so-called mystical insight."[5] In order to keep the focus of his novel on the hero rather than the system, Koestler employs an unusually vivid, tactile imagery, as well as the characteristic confessional technique of the double.

5. Peter Viereck, *"Darkness at Noon* Revisited," foreword to Koestler, *Darkness at Noon.*

The imagery of *Darkness at Noon* is designed to translate the hero's political and philosophical struggles into physical and emotional terms which emphasize their relation to basic human problems. Rubashov suffers from an excruciating toothache throughout the narrative, indicating the very real pain which he undergoes in his abstract thoughts. A dialogue about the "vivisection morality" of the Communist system is brought to life in an explicit account of a man killing a cat with his bare hands. Rubashov remembers Arlova, the simple girl he betrayed, by her pleasant scent. He tries to disclaim responsibility for that betrayal by rationalizing about the good of the party, but his persistent feeling of guilt is revealed through the symbol of the wastebucket in his cell: "The bucket stank; its vapors had replaced the scent of Arlova" (p. 122).

Koestler's extensive use of doubles also helps him to depict the hero's mental conflict in effective dramatic terms. Three of these doubles exist in Rubashov's past, and his memory of them leads him toward an awareness of his own guilt. Three others are his contemporaries and serve to illuminate aspects of his own condition. Finally, there is the young officer Gletkin, the demonic tormentor who forces Rubashov to endure the most painful stages of his self-examination. A study of these doubles will illuminate the significance of Rubashov's confession as an important human drama which transcends the specific question of Communist ideology.

The doubles in Rubashov's past are three former comrades whom he has sacrificed to the needs of the party, just as he is about to be sacrificed to the party's revised conception of those needs. As he condemned them, Rubashov felt only a vague sorrow; in his own cell, he is suddenly able to identify fully with them, as he himself faces the terrible experience of being victimized by the party to which he has devoted his life.

The first of these doubles is Richard, a nervous nineteen-year-old who has dared to contradict official propaganda and distribute his own leaflets. Rubashov meets him in a museum, and the image which dominates the scene is a pen drawing of the *Pietà*. The sketch is partially hidden by his comrade's head, so Rubashov can see only the thin outstretched hands of the Madonna—delicate symbols of mercy. Richard stammers his report and awaits Rubashov's verdict in a posture which prefigures Rubashov's own fate: "He sat as one who had confessed and was waiting for the father-confessor's sentence" (p. 43). Rubashov's answer shatters the frail hope of mercy which the *Pietà* proffers. "The Party can never be mistaken," he says. He expels the stunned youth. On the way out, he forgets his earlier desire to examine the entire pen drawing.

The episode with Richard emphasizes the party's denial of both individual thought and such an "illogical" value as mercy.[6] Rubashov's meeting with the second double in his past, a dockworker named Little Loewy, focuses on another aspect of his Communist belief, the assertion that the end justifies any means including "vivisection morality." It also points out the need for even the most devoted party member to change his views in accordance with every capricious shift in the policy of his leaders; Loewy's failure to do so and his subsequent demise prefigure Rubashov's own execution by the younger generation of rulers. These ideological factors are again portrayed in vivid physical action.

Little Loewy tells Rubashov that he spent most of his life running from prison to prison in two different countries. Although the party headquarters in both countries refused to accept him without credentials, Loewy's fierce dedication endured. Determined to keep alive and maintain his usefulness to the cause, he

6. In *What Is To Be Done?* (New York, International Publishers, 1929), Lenin emphasizes the dangers of individual thought and any "spontaneity" of action. "Our task, the task of Social Democracy, is to *combat spontaneity*," he writes (p. 41). Later, he repeats, "The Economists and the modern terrorists spring from a common root, namely, *subservience to spontaneity*" (p. 73).

even took up "the cat trade"; Rubashov recalls his description of "the rather unpleasant operation" this involved: "It was the quickest if one grasped the cat's ears in one hand, and its tail in the other, and broke its back over one's knee. The first few times one was seized by moments of nausea: later on one got used to it" (p. 65). The deep impression which this account makes on Rubashov becomes immediately apparent. He has been sent to Loewy's country to announce a trade agreement which will cancel the dockworkers' fervent strike plans and crush their fanatical faith in the party. He is suddenly struck by a hideous vision of his own destructive role: "He could not get over the obsession that he must take Little Loewy by the ears and legs and break him over his knee, deformed shoulder and all" (p. 67). When the workers do desert the party and Little Loewy hangs himself, Rubashov again claims immunity behind the Communist creed, yet his dream lingers, adding another element to his vague dissatisfaction with his system and with himself.

Finally, the docile Arlova unwittingly confronts Rubashov with the awesome magnitude of his personal responsibility. During their first night together, she tells him calmly, "You will always be able to do what you like with me" (p. 104). From the moment this simple statement is uttered, Rubashov begins to notice "a curious feeling of guilt." He suppresses this feeling while he allows her to be executed, seeking to shift responsibility for her death from himself onto the party. Only when he enters his cell and faces the fate foreshadowed by Arlova—faithful submission rewarded with death—can Rubashov bring himself to accept the reality of that "curious feeling."

The hero's examination of his past takes him several, partial, tentative steps away from the rigid party definitions of good and evil by introducing a heightened sense of the importance of individual responsibility. The subtle change in his thinking is apparent in one brief exchange with the monarchist in the next cell. Amused at his neighbor's display of hatred for him, Rubashov thinks coldly, "How many of yours have I shot, I wonder? . . . Between seventy and a hundred. What of it?" (p. 56) In his next words, however, he reveals for the first time that he feels sorry about an earlier action; the murders of reactionaries, he says, "lay on a different plane to a case like Richard's." Then he approaches a more sweeping heresy, a sense of responsibility to all men, which recalls the elder Zossima in *The Brothers Kara- mazov* and which constitutes the antithesis of Communist moral- ity: "Do I perhaps owe you the fare all the same?" he silently asks the monarchist. "Must one also pay for deeds which were right and necessary?" The fact that he is willing to ask this ques- tion at all indicates the extent of the transformation taking place within Rubashov. However, the content of the question—with its vaguely implied doubt about the Communist definitions of the words "right" and "necessary"—simultaneously shows how far Rubashov remains from full self-perception. His disillusionment is still peripheral; it has not yet penetrated his consciousness to a point at which he will directly question the most fundamental truths of his system.

Turning from the episodes of his past to the nature of his present existence, we can learn more about the nature of Koest- ler's hero. *Darkness at Noon,* written in France in the German language by a Hungarian-born author, is sometimes placed in the context of French literature, and Rubashov does resemble the intellectual heroes of the French confessional novels. Although his mental powers have been developed by experience rather than formal education, they are far-ranging enough to dominate the novel. In fact, since *Darkness at Noon* is primarily an account of the hero's thinking, it is worth examining the manner in which Koestler presents those thoughts, particularly through his modifi- cation of the technique of the double.

The main uses of the double, as seen in Dostoevsky and other confessional writers, have been the illumination of certain sup- pressed facets of the hero's consciousness and the portrayal of important elements in his confession. Koestler also uses the device in this way during Rubashov's recollections of his past. The three characters who reflect the hero in the present, however, remain more distant from both his psychology and his confession. Their function is to evoke a mood, a sense of age and decay, of lost bearings in a world of flux. Expressed directly by the hero, these ideas would be self-pity; reflected in the three characters around him, they form a sensitive picture of a faded and condemned generation.

The first of these modified doubles is the least complex. Vassilij, the old porter of the building in which Rubashov lives, appears only at the beginning and end of the novel in a function reminiscent of a classical chorus. Although he never speaks to the hero during the novel, Vassilij is identified with him by the scar he received while fighting in Rubashov's regiment during the Civil War. Gradually, the old man has lost contact with the changing world in which Rubashov lives; his old hero's speeches, read to him by his daughter, have become "long and difficult to understand," in contrast to the straightforward and delightful battlefield oaths which Vassilij recalls. This mood of change, combined with the image of the old porter cowering before Rubashov's arresting officers, opens the novel on a note of lost heroism.

In his reappearance near the end of the novel, Vassilij escapes his long state of confusion to evoke a last, bitter, choric comment. As his daughter, a loyal party worker, derides Rubashov, he interrupts: "A lot you know about it." The girl glances at her father with an expression that forces Vassilij to face the decline of his generation: "Each time she gave him that peculiar glance Vassilij was reminded that he was in Vera Vassilijovna's way, who wanted to have the porter's lodge for herself" (p. 206). Standing amid the terrible destruction at the end of *Antigone,* the Sophoclean chorus ironically concludes, "So wisdom comes to the old."[7] Vassilij, turning his face to the wall with a resigned

7. Sophocles, *Antigone,* trans. Elizabeth Wyckoff (Chicago, University of Chicago Press [Grene and Lattimore series], 1954), p. 204.

"Amen," presents an equally striking image of the grim wisdom which awaits the old under the Communist system.

A more comical reflection of the state of Rubashov's generation is offered in the figure of "Rip Van Winkle," the old man who returns to the Soviet "Promised Land" after twenty years in a foreign jail and finds Russia so changed that he is arrested as a reactionary within two weeks. Undaunted, he simply concludes that he was put on the wrong train and sent to an enemy country; thus, he maintains his faith in the party until his execution. "Rip" is clearly a symbol of the alienation of the old guard from the changing Communist system, but he also highlights another aspect of Rubashov's situation. His blind, unwavering faith in the party is humorous because it is so extreme; yet a similar feeling, tempered by events and careful thought, is present in Rubashov. It is this feeling which produces the conflict between disillusionment and loyalty in the hero and preserves his determination to rebuild his crumbling system.

Old Vassilij and "Rip Van Winkle" are, strictly speaking, symbols rather than doubles. They do not contribute directly to the hero's self-examination, but they embellish the portrayal of his thoughts and moods. It is the third member of this trio of contemporaries, Rubashov's captor Ivanov, who begins to lead him into the deeper psychological phase of his confession. The tone of the meetings with Ivanov is set by an image which emphasizes the hero's decline. "Instead of the old portraits a light patch shone from the wallpaper," a stark symbol of the liquidation of the old Communist leaders. This light patch also recalls Rubashov's meeting with Richard in the museum. At that time, Rubashov refused the mercy shown in the drawing of the *Pietà* on the wall and condemned the boy; now, when he himself needs mercy or help, there is no picture at all to which he can appeal. Ivanov feels a distant sympathy for his old comrade, but he has chosen to accept the changing party system, so he is obliged to interrogate Rubashov until he confesses. In their conversations, the two men are drawn closer to one another until Ivanov's role as a double is explicitly declared. He tells the hero: *"You are afraid of me.* Because my way of thinking and of arguing is your own, and you are afraid of the echo in your own head. In a moment you will be calling out: Get thee behind me, Satan" (p. 130). And Rubashov ruefully admits that "every sentence . . . did in fact evoke an echo in him."

In a brilliant ironic twist, however, Ivanov is snatched away just as he has begun to penetrate Rubashov's mind; he is accused of laxity and executed, compounding the hero's awareness of his own impending doom. The irony of Ivanov's demise accentuates the pervasive ironic sense expressed in the fate of Vassilij, "Rip," and Ivanov. All three of these men have, like Rubashov himself, embraced the Communist system in search of some certainty within a confused world. At the end of their lives, however, that certainty becomes a curse; their rigid system speeds them toward death, as the young, like Vera Vassilijovna, wait anxiously for them to be out of the way.

Rubashov's interrogation is taken over by Gletkin, prototype of the new party leader, who sees all of life as "a matter of constitution." It is Gletkin who becomes the ultimate extension of the double in *Darkness at Noon* and gives truth to Ivanov's prophecy that Rubashov would cry out against Satan. The striking contrast between Rubashov's earlier interrogations with Ivanov and his climactic confrontation with Gletkin is expressed through the metaphor of light. Instead of the light patch on Ivanov's wall—symbol of a yearning for past glory—Rubashov is faced with a room full of glaring lights, stripping him of all protection against the pain of his present situation. His captor is no longer an image of the party he has served, but an embodiment of the brutal new generation. "You consequential brute in the uniform we created," Rubashov thinks, "barbarian of the new age which is now starting" (p. 159). Gradually, however, Rubashov is forced into the realization that he and his comrades created not only the uniform but the man within it. Gletkin becomes, like Ivan Karamazov's devil, a grotesque reflection of the worst aspects of the hero's own life and beliefs, compelling Rubashov to admit his own failure. The parallels between this scene and "Ivan's Nightmare" are striking.

Both scenes occur previous to trials, and both Gletkin and Ivan's devil taunt their victims about the impossibility of exercising free will at those trials. "All my stupid ideas," Ivan cries to his tormentor, "you present to me now as something new! . . . How can my soul beget a flunkey like you?"[8] Rubashov is also compelled to acknowledge his double as a child of his own spirit: "Flesh of [our] flesh, grown independent and become insensible. Had not Gletkin acknowledged himself to be the spiritual heir of Ivanov and the old intelligentsia?" (p. 192) Ivan tells his visitor, "I'm bored with you agonizingly and insufferably,"[9] but his attempts to drive the devil away are futile, and he is forced to listen to the full recitation of the "poems" which composed his own system. Rubashov experiences comparable anguish in the endless hours under the bright lamps, as Gletkin reads mechanically from his prisoner's diary, "as though a confession, intended only for the anonymous priest, had been registered on a gramophone record, which was now repeating it in its cracked voice" (p. 197).

The one crucial difference between these two scenes lies in the reaction of the hero to his double's destruction of his system. Ivan had accepted his guilt only a few hours before his "nightmare," in his talk with another double, Smerdyakov, but the destructive force of the devil obscures his resolution to absolve that guilt, and he sinks into madness. Rubashov confronts the primary symbol of his own guilt during the interrogation by Gletkin. In his series of accusations of imagined and exaggerated crimes, Gletkin stumbles on an actual one:

> "So it is possible that citizen Arlova was innocent?"
> "It is possible," said Rubashov with a last remainder of

8. Dostoevsky, *The Brothers Karamazov*, p. 588.
9. Ibid., p. 587.

irony which lay on his tongue like a taste of blood and gall.
". . . And was executed as a consequence of the lying declaration you made, with the object of saving your head?"
"That is about it," said Rubashov. . . .
"And after all that you demand to be treated with consideration?" Gletkin's voice went on, with the same brutal cor-
rectness. . . .
Rubashov gave up his efforts to keep his head straight.
(pp. 164–65)

When his interrogation finally ends, Rubashov's beliefs have been
reduced to chaos; only his perception of guilt remains. Unlike
Ivan, he does not allow the collapse of his system to smother this
single positive element of his awareness, the sense of personal
responsibility. Thus, he can still see "the gliding, swerving play
of the birds, high above the machine-gun turret." He has not lost
his determination to resist the forces of disintegration, and,
equipped with his new self-awareness, he resumes his search for
order.

The continuation of this unrelenting search distinguishes
Koestler's hero from Ivan and, indeed, from every confessional
hero we have discussed. *Darkness at Noon* has brought an unwavering hope into the uncertain secular world of the modern
novel, and that hope has survived its severest test. In the wake
of the monumental failure of one system of order, the spirit of
hope affirms the possibility of finding another, better one. It is
clear, however, that Koestler will reject any more simple, external
solutions based on logic and "cause and effect." Rubashov decides
that "the hours which remained belonged to that silent partner,
whose realm started just where logical thought ended . . . the
'grammatical fiction.' " When he taps the word "I" in code on
the cell wall, "it dies without resonance"; it can never be recognized in the world of the party. He realizes that he must seek fulfillment of the self beyond that world, in the "oceanic sense."

111

At last Rubashov sees the missing factor in the Communist equation:

> Why had not the Public Prosecutor asked him: "Defendant Rubashov, what about the infinite?" He would not have been able to answer—and there, there lay the real source of his guilt. . . . Could there be a greater? (p. 214)

Like that of all modern confessional heroes, the final perception achieved by Rubashov remains incomplete. His death conveys a tremendous sense of waste; his awareness of the infinite has come too late to balance his forty years of devotion to a false religion. His execution is swift and final, and his last thought is one of bitter disillusionment. He envies Moses, who had at least been allowed to see his Promised Land. "But he, Nicolas Salmanovitch Rubashov, had not been taken to the top of the mountain; and wherever he looked, he saw nothing but desert and the darkness of night" (p. 222).

This conclusion culminates the disintegration of the hero's system which has occurred throughout *Darkness at Noon,* but it cannot obscure the positive theme of the novel. In his final thought before the arrival of his executioners, Rubashov envisions a new party of the distant future:

> Perhaps they will teach that the tenet is wrong which says that a man is the quotient of one million divided by one million, and will introduce a new kind of arithmetic based on multiplication: on the joining of a million individuals to form a new entity which, no longer an amorphous mass, will develop a consciousness and an individuality of its own, with an "oceanic feeling" increased a millionfold. (pp. 217–18)

This vague and distant vision outlives its creator, to stand in opposition to the assertion of Jean-Baptiste Clamence that "It will always be too late" and to affirm the possibility of regeneration in the disintegrated modern world.

In contrast to *Darkness at Noon,* which introduces one complete system, examines its collapse, and then tentatively offers another one, Golding's *Free Fall* presents only fragments of systems. Its hero begins with no system at all and ends with only a hint of one. Yet, in describing man's approach to meaning rather than his scrutiny of its elements, Golding examines another important aspect of the modern confession.

Superficially, the hero of the novel is a success, a boy from the slums who has become a famous artist and now lives on Paradise Hill. Yet he calls himself "a burning amateur, torn by the irrational and incoherent, searching and self-condemned" (p. 5). Unlike most confessional characters, who are never sure what kind of perception they will find, Sammy Mountjoy clearly defines the goals of his self-examination. Foremost among them are the questions which are introduced at the beginning of the second and third paragraphs and repeated throughout the novel —"When did I lose my freedom?" and "How did I lose my freedom?" The lost quality of freedom is described as a tangible element, like "the taste of potatoes," yet it stands for broader philosophical problems than Sammy admits, directing his confession toward a fuller consideration of the meaning of sin and guilt.

In addition to seeking this one point in his life, "the decision made freely that cost me my freedom," the hero of *Free Fall* is approaching a kind of personal religion. In the disintegration following the loss of freedom, "all patterns have broken, one after another. Life is random and evil unpunished." Sammy wants to rebuild a pattern and restore order and justice; in doing so, he hopes to give meaning to his divided existence, to find "the connection between the little boy clear as spring water, and the man like a stagnant pool" (p. 9). Like all confessional heroes, Sammy

Mountjoy seeks a perception which is deeply personal; he is concerned with an internal system of order. He expresses the Underground Man's statement that "I am writing for myself alone" in one of the visual images which characterize his narrative:

> I have hung all systems on the wall like a row of useless hats. They do not fit. They come in from outside, they are suggested patterns, some dull and some of great beauty. But I have lived enough of my life to require a pattern that fits over everything I know. . . . You know of me, Samuel Mountjoy, I hang in the Tate. You would forgive me any hat. I could be a cannibal. But I want to wear a hat in private. I want to understand. (pp. 6–7)

The first paragraph of *Free Fall* is a remarkable prelude to both the components and the overall significance of the hero's confession:

> I have walked by stalls in the market-place where books, dog-eared and faded from their purple, have burst with a white hosanna. I have seen people crowned with a double crown, holding in either hand the crook and flail, the power and the glory. I have understood how the scar becomes a star, I have felt the flake of fire fall, miraculous and pentecostal. My yesterdays walk with me. They keep step, they are grey faces that peer over my shoulder. (p. 5)

This passage contains a reference to almost every memory which the hero will explore during his confession. There is Philip Arnold, master of duplicity and minister of the government; the scar inflicted by the verger's fist on the altar; the stars of Nick Shales' scientific world; the purple of long suffering and the white hosannas promised by many systems and finally achieved in the "resurrection" at the prison camp. More important, this opening paragraph introduces the crucial problem of Sammy's condition. It is full of images of blazing light and revelation, but it ends on a statement of guilt. As long as the faces of his past are grey and shadowy, Sammy cannot transform his isolated moments of revelation into a full understanding of his own life; and as long as he lacks that understanding, his "white hosannas" can bring no purgation or redemption, but only a more acute consciousness of the dark confusion which surrounds them.

Ian Gregor and Mark Kinkead-Weekes are among the few critics who have realized the importance of this carefully fugal paragraph in *Free Fall*. They admit that a first response might be to find it "unbearably pretentious, overblown Dylan Thomas," but they conclude:

> To get the point of this first paragraph is to get the point of the whole book. Sammy has already some insight into the truth of the fall, the judgment and the transfiguration of the earth through tears; but in seeking to realize the myth in its full implications in his own life, what he is looking for is forgiveness and reconciliation. . . . The "monstrous consciousness" that we set out to explore is the experience of a split world, in which spiritual insight has only entered to condemn.[10]

After the tightly organized presentation of the central goals and themes of his confession in the opening pages, Sammy Mountjoy begins the examination of his past. He ranges back and forth through what he calls the "shuffle fold and coil" of time, often juxtaposing events from his innocent childhood with others that occur after his "fall." As the grey faces of his past take on shape and color, he approaches the discovery of his moment of sin. Five times, after the accounts of events in his youth, Sammy asks, "Here?" Each time he answers himself, "Not here." After the final perception of the moment in which he lost his freedom, Sammy repeats his question; it is followed by a profound silence.

10. Ian Gregor and Mark Kinkead-Weekes, "The Strange Case of Mr. Golding and His Critics," *Twentieth Century* (February 1960), p. 119.

The method in which Sammy describes his early childhood recalls the explanation of Saul Bellow's hero, Augie March, that "All the influences were lined up waiting for me. I was born, and there they were to form me, which is why I tell you more of them than of myself."[11] As a boy growing up in the slums, Sammy is innocent and happy, being shaped by external forces. He finds contentment in the "warm darkness" of his mother and the entertaining lies of an older girl named Evie. "Rotten Row," he recalls, "was roaring and warm, simple and complex, individual and . . . strangely happy" (p. 33). Even as he emphasizes the depth of his happiness, however, Sammy sees the shadow of the sin to come:

> My mother was as near a whore as makes no matter and Evie was a congenital liar. Yet if they would only exist there was nothing more I wanted. I remember the quality of this relationship so vividly that I am almost tempted into an aphorism: love selflessly and you cannot come to harm. But then I remember some things that came after. (p. 33)

Among the "things that came after" are Sammy's two friends, Johnny Spragg and Philip Arnold. With Johnny, Sammy develops his spirit of adventure and daring, but their mischief does not rob them of their innocence. At the end of his account of Johnny, Sammy says, "I am still looking for the beginning of responsibility." Philip Arnold, on the other hand, is alien to the child's world of innocence. "He knew about people," says Sammy; Gregor and Kinkead-Weekes say of Philip, "Because he is conscious he never was a child."[12] A coward himself, Philip incites Sammy to rob smaller boys of their fagcards in the school lavatory, precipitating the first crisis of Sammy's approach to guilt. He is caught and brought to the principal, fully expecting punishment. "This was a humane and enlightened school," however,

11. Saul Bellow, *The Adventures of Augie March* (Greenwich, Conn., Crest, 1965), p. 46.
12. Gregor and Kinkead-Weekes, p. 119.

so the principal "let the cane stay in the corner and my guilt stay on my back" (p. 52). For the first time, Sammy asks his central question: "Is this the point I am looking for?" But his guilt is the passing guilt of a child; his crime, after all, was barely intentional, prompted by his devious friend. He answers, "No. Not here."

"But this was not the profoundest thing that Philip achieved for me," says the hero with rueful irony. He describes how Philip goads him into desecrating the altar, leading him to the end of the blind trust of his earliest years. "The universe exploded at my right hand side" in the blow of the verger; somewhere in the "singing and roaring" of his pain, Sammy hears the sound of the closing church door as Philip slips away. The finality of its "Wubb, Wuff" marks the end of passive contentment for the child.

In the next stage of his life, which centers around the rectory and the school, Sammy's outlook becomes more cautious, his perception more sophisticated. His new guardian, Father Watts-Watt, repels him ("Talking with him was like a nightmare ride on a giraffe"), but, for the first time, Sammy shows the ability to resist the influence of another person. He arrives at an extraordinarily mature judgment about all the people he meets in the hospital and rectory:

> As I progressed from person to person the fantasy changed in character but remained substantially the same in relation to the teller. They were all trying to adjust the brute blow of the fist that daily existence dealt them till it became a caress. (p. 162)

As this statement indicates, Father Watts-Watt represents the antithesis of the confessional hero, a man struggling to avoid the reality of his being. In addition to this contrast to the hero, however, he is also a kind of double. "He was incapable of approaching a child straight because of the ingrown and festering desires that poisoned him," says Sammy (p. 163). In this, he reflects the dark and confused drives which plague the hero in the events leading up to his fall. The most dramatic scene which occurs in

117

the rectory also serves as a prelude to Sammy's experience at the prison camp. Scared of the dark, Sammy crawls from his bed and climbs up to take a bulb from the ceiling light. Just as his hands touch the light, Father Watts-Watt opens the door and flicks the switch. The terrified youth stands momentarily exposed in the glare, as he will later stand before Halde; then he leaps back into bed. He "huddled there sitting knees up," just as, in the prison cell, he "cared only to protect my privates." In these two instances, Father Watts-Watt, the man who cannot recognize his interior being, foreshadows the depths to which Sammy will sink before he comes to a recognition of his own inner self.

While he lives in the rectory, Sammy says, "There was perhaps still time; but no one told me, no one knew what we might see and how easily we might lose the faculty" (p. 154). This statement indicates that the young man is desperately seeking guidance. His search leads him to the two schoolteachers, Rowena Pringle and Nick Shales, "the virgin and the water-carrier." These characters offer the polar alternatives in his choice of a system by which to live. Initially, Sammy's innate love of brilliant images and colors draws him toward the miracles and adventures of Miss Pringle's biblical world, rather than the "dreary rationalistic universe" of Nick Shales. But Miss Pringle ultimately offers Sammy nothing; her failure is expressed in one succinct statement: "Miss Pringle never touched anyone" (p. 195). Nick, on the other hand, convinces Sammy that "he wanted us to understand." Furthermore, Nick is forthright and honest, while "the so-respectable school-marm with her clean fingers was eaten up with secret desires and passions" (p. 214) which render her as incapable of communication as Father Watts-Watt. Sammy's crucial choice of a system is dominated by these characters rather than their ideas, as he admits in one cryptic statement:

> For an instant out of time, the two worlds existed side by side. . . . To give up the burning bush, the water on the

rock, the spittle on the eyes was to give up a portion of myself, a dark and inward and fruitful portion. Yet looking at me from the bush was the fat and freckled face of Miss Pringle. The other world, the cool and reasonable, was home to the friendly face of Nick Shales. I do not believe that rational choice stood any chance of exercise. I believe that my child's mind was made up for me as a choice of good and wicked fairies. (p. 217)

Even in this weighty decision, Sammy's lack of "rational choice" absolves him from the full guilt which would destroy freedom. When, immediately afterward, he asks, "Here?" he can still answer, "Not here." Nevertheless, this choice is the prelude to his sin, for just as Father Watts-Watt's suppression of all sexual drives left them unchecked and uncomprehended in the hero, Nick's attempt to ignore sex forces Sammy to resolve his compulsions on his own. Those compulsions rise to an unbearable pitch as he moves closer to their object, Beatrice Ifor. "Help me," he cries. "I have gone mad. I want to be you" (p. 105). But Beatrice, so passive that her most enthusiastic reaction to anything is "Maybe," cannot help. He tries one final approach to Nick, but the teacher "shut me up violently" and becomes forever more a "fallen angel" to Sammy. In desperation, Sammy grasps the only shred of advice which is offered, the headmaster's paradoxical counsel: "If you want something enough you can always get it provided you are willing to make the appropriate sacrifice. . . . But what you get is never quite what you thought" (p. 235). He resolves to sacrifice "Everything." At this point, the decisive question is repeated, "Here?" No answer follows. Sammy now understands where he has lost his freedom, but he must continue his exploration of his past to find out why this sacrifice led him to disaster. The answer lies in the nature of Beatrice herself, to which we will return after following the hero's narrative through the next stage of his life.

Once freedom has been lost, Sammy's life assumes all the characteristics of an uncontrolled and precipitous fall. His recollections of the conquest and destruction of Beatrice are marked by recurrent statements that he is powerless to stop himself, powerless to stay with her, and, most important, powerless to choose good and evil in the relationship. "Insensibly I drifted rather than went deliberately into the last cruel effort to meet her," he says. His long-sought prize proves to be an exquisite disappointment: "And then Beatrice of four years' fever lay back obediently, closed her eyes and placed one clenched fist bravely on her forehead as though she were about to be injected for T.A.B." (p. 117).

Sammy's sexual frustration drives him to an animated affair with Taffy, and his need for a belief to replace Nick Shales' crumbling system leads to Communism. His account of his experiences in the party emphasizes his increasing awareness that no limited external system can save him; the episode also presents several remarkable parallels between Golding and Koestler. Rubashov's meeting with Little Loewy and his helplessness against the party's "vivisection morality" are recalled by Sammy's description of his flight from Beatrice. He remembers seeing a cat that has been run over and is screaming with pain: "I could do nothing but run away. I could not kill the cat to stop it suffering" (p. 131). Sammy derides the party's membership of frustrated intellectuals and the wide gap between theory and practice: "Workers of the world, unite! We had a worker . . . our jewel, Dai Reece." But Dai has a tendency to be "appallingly bourgeois" and must be disciplined frequently by the schoolteacher who leads the cell. Brombert points out that Koestler also ridiculed the Communists' image of the idealized model worker:

> Koestler describes the cult of the "prolo," this obsession of all Communist intellectuals; how they attempted to imitate the archetypal, broad-shouldered, square-jawed worker of the Putilov factories, gave up wearing ties, made sure their

nails were dirty and did their utmost to castrate their thinking.[13]

Clearly, this kind of organized self-delusion cannot retard Sammy's downward rush toward the prison cell.

The "nationless words" of Dr. Halde cut Sammy loose from all his remaining ties with order. Halde is clearly a double of the hero. He implies that he, too, has sacrificed his own freedom by choosing Nazism and emphasizes the price of such a sacrifice: "I made my choice with much difficulty but I have made it. Perhaps it was the last choice I shall ever make. Accept such international immortality, Mr. Mountjoy, and all unpleasantnesses are possible to man" (p. 140). He laughs at Sammy's objections "as if I were a child again, making a mistake in my classwork." The significance of this allusion to the past becomes more apparent when, under the influence of the "pentecostal fire," Sammy immediately locates the setting of his sin: "Back among the flowers and smell of cloakrooms, among the exercise books and savage emotions, back among the rewards and penalties, back with the sense of life going on like that forever" (p. 192).

Halde is more than a reflection of the hero's life, however. His psychological powers allow him to claim, "I can get inside your skin"; and it is only from within that perception can reach Sammy. Halde's power over his prisoner becomes vividly clear as the interrogation progresses. When the Nazi first describes his theory of "international immorality," Sammy hastens to deny its relevance to his own condition: "What's all that got to do with me?" Within moments, however, his mind has accepted Halde's thought as its own: "I could see this war as the ghastly and ferocious play of children who having made a wrong choice or a whole series of them were now helplessly tormenting each other because a wrong use of freedom has lost them their freedom" (p. 151). This striking progression illuminates the full meaning of Sammy's statement that he "was given the capacity to see" by

13. Brombert, *The Intellectual Hero*, p. 154.

Dr. Halde. When the interrogation ends, Sammy walks out of the office "in an awful trance of obedience" and is led to his cell.

As a double, Halde is very similar to his Satanic counterparts, Ivan's visitor and Gletkin. Rubashov repeatedly calls Gletkin "the tempter," and Halde sees himself in analogous terms: "I have taken you up to a pinnacle of the temple and shown you the whole earth" (p. 147). He scorns Sammy's protests—"What rights have you?"—in the tone of Gletkin's contemptuous question, *"You* demand to be treated with consideration?" Like those other two doubles, Halde manages to destroy all remnants of order and peace in the mind of the hero and leaves him in a profound state of isolation in which he is compelled to acknowledge the meaning of the self.

In the early stages of his experience in the cell, it appears that Sammy will follow Ivan's path into madness; but in his resurrection he emerges with a vision that is, in some ways, even more hopeful than that of Rubashov. For Sammy is not at the end of life. He has time to use the "new mode of knowing" which Halde has given him and to apply his newly discovered "vital morality" to the reconstruction of meaning in his own life. If he succeeds, he may place a living reality where Rubashov could see only a dream of the future. On this promising note, Golding directs our attention back over Sammy's life to seek a positive "pattern" amid the disintegration.

However, Golding, like all the confessional novelists we have discussed, denies his hero the fulfillment of his momentary religious perception. The blazing hopes of the prison camp resurrection are tempered by an ironic reality. Sammy probes deeply into the "two worlds" of his existence and achieves a clear perception of both, but the crucial missing element of his pattern eludes him. "There is no bridge," he admits on the final page of the novel.

A closer examination of Sammy's "two worlds" elucidates both the pattern he seeks and the true nature of his fall. He is painfully aware of the split which robs his life of meaning: "I can love the child in the garden, on the airfield, in Rotten Row," he says, "because he is not I. He is another person" (p. 46). That child is innocent; the adult Sammy is tainted with guilt. They are thus relegated to two separate worlds.

The impossibility of crossing back into the first world is shown most emphatically in Sammy's attempt to contact the central characters of that child's world. Like Michel in Gide's *The Immoralist,* Sammy confronts utter futility in his effort to retrace the course of his earlier actions. The three people to whom he returns are strangers, totally divorced from the characters he once knew. Nick Shales, prophet of the self-contained physical world, is in a hospital, "dying of a tired heart." Rowena Pringle, destroyer of a "dark and fruitful" part of Sammy's childhood world, happily and irrelevantly declares herself "a teeny-weeny bit responsible" for her pupil's superficial success in life. Beatrice Ifor, the fascinating and irresistible girl whose very being the fervent schoolboy had wanted so much to penetrate and share, is found in an insane asylum—"the image of a betrayed woman, of outraged and helpless innocence." She is as remote and unapproachable as the idiot child Minnie had once been. The striking parallel between Minnie's disgrace in the nursery school and the scene in the insane asylum leads directly to the crucial role of Beatrice in the novel and, through Beatrice, to the full meaning of Sammy's fall. Both Minnie and Beatrice express their utter helplessness by "pissing . . . on the . . . shoes" of a visitor. (Sammy's shoes replace the "nice lady's" shoes, but the phrase otherwise remains significantly constant.) This realizes the hero's haunting dream of the "waters rising round him." The dream thus connects the most horrifying elements of both Sammy's worlds and becomes a negative, acutely ironic mockery of the positive bridge for which he is looking.

The relation of these characters also extends to Sammy's reaction to them. With her mind hidden from him, Minnie "was an appearance, to be accepted like anything else. . . . Life was permanent and inevitable in this shape" (p. 34). When he fails to reach Beatrice's internal being, Sammy tries to make her permanent in the same visual way, by painting her portrait. The futility of this approach is clear even during Sammy's innocence. In the art class, he manages only once to capture on paper "the great eyes, grey and lucent" and the face of an "angel of the annunciation"—only to watch Philip Arnold sign the sketch and earn the smile which Sammy so desperately craves. After innocence is lost, his drawings of Beatrice become not merely futile but terrible, a representation of "her exploitation and my self-contempt." He tells her, "I shan't paint your face. I just want your body," and he even adds a glaring electric light to the oil reproduction of his shame. That painting is hanging in a gallery, an ironic symbol of Sammy's "success," while he visits the insane asylum and finds that his image has indeed become horribly and mockingly permanent: "Beatrice sat, looking at the wall, looking at nothing. Her face was in the shadow of her body" (p. 242). In her ruined state, Beatrice has become a nightmarish distortion of the pattern and the order which Sammy had hoped to find. Yet her negative impact forces us back to a realization of her positive meaning—of what she might have been if Sammy had not destroyed her.

Almost every proper name in *Free Fall* implies something about the character it identifies, but none is so crucial as "Beatrice Ifor." The girl is, as Gregor and Kinkead-Weekes suggest, "a *fusion* of the spirit and the body . . . both Beatrice and I-for"[14]; in other words, she is the potential bridge between Sammy's two worlds. But the young boy, torn by the contradictory worlds of his two teachers, each of whom denies the existence of the other's system, cannot see the possibility of fusion; he sees Beatrice in the light implied by another reading of her name, "If-or" and thus feels compelled to choose one of the two worlds. Repelled by

14. Gregor and Kinkead-Weekes, p. 122.

Miss Pringle and attracted to Nick, who finds "no place for spirit in his cosmos," he ignores the spiritual side of the girl and grasps only the "I-for," the self-centered, exploitative lust. He upsets the balance and destroys the bridge.

Herein lies the full significance of his loss of freedom. He has chosen to shut out a part of the complex world and embrace a simplified half-truth as a substitute for the full consciousness of existence. One dominant theme of the confessional novel is the inadequacy of such "simple solutions"—from the Grand Inquisitor through Jean-Baptiste Clamence, from Ivan Karamazov through the "defective saints" of Rubashov's party. Golding does not spare Sammy Mountjoy from the effects of his error—the denial of freedom and the "fall."

Ultimately, the reader of *Free Fall* is challenged to find another bridge—a reconciliation of the blazingly affirmative vision of the prison camp with the final bleak realization that "There is no bridge" in Sammy's existence. Golding offers one clue to this solution on the final page of the novel. Sammy walks out of his cell expecting to meet his judge but finds pity instead. Halde has been replaced, and the commandant apologizes for Sammy's punishment. A soldier asks, "Captain Mountjoy. Have you heard?" and he answers, "I heard." What he has "heard" is the voice of his own being and perhaps also a voice of absolution. He is an image of fallen man, unable to undo his sin; but he has suffered for it and sees a hope of redemption.

The position of *Free Fall* in the context of all Golding's work also illuminates the religious vision of the novel. His first two novels, *Lord of the Flies* and *The Inheritors,* are parables portraying the evil inherent in man's nature; in them, the author employs images of man's origins, in childhood and in prehistory, to illustrate man's swift and inevitable loss of innocence. *Pincher Martin* turns from the nature of evil itself and focuses on its spiritual consequences. The hero, shipwrecked on a barren rock, seems to survive for several days through a monumental assertion of will. "I will impose my routine on this rock," he says. On the last page of the novel, we learn that he has been dead all along, and the routine he has imposed is a self-created hell. The final page emphasizes the terrible irony of Martin's earlier conversation with his "hallucination" of God (a striking derivation from Dostoevsky's hallucinatory doubles). In that exchange, the hero shouts, "I have created you and I can create my own heaven." The old man answers, "You have created it."[15]

The idea that man creates his own hell is carried into the prison cell of *Free Fall.* "Why do you torment yourself?" Sammy says. "Why do you do their work for them?" (p. 183) But Sammy Mountjoy is given the power to escape from the hell he creates and even, "between the understood huts, among jewels and music," to glimpse at heaven.[16] Although the heaven fades and he can never regain the innocence that preceded the fall, he can return to an existence enriched by "a new mode of knowing."

In a private letter to one critic, Golding explained the idea behind one of the symbols of hell in *Pincher Martin:* "The cellar . . . represents more than childhood terrors; a whole philosophy in fact—suggesting that God is the thing we turn away from into life."[17] It is this kind of philosophy which illuminates the essen-

15. William Golding, *Pincher Martin* (New York, Capricorn, 1956), pp. 174–75.

16. It seems that this kind of brief and fiery "glimpse" of heaven is the most meaningful approach to religion for man in Golding's world. His most recent novel, *The Spire* (New York, Harcourt, Brace and World, 1964), describes the dean of a cathedral who seeks to make the church "even more glorious than before" and brings ruin on himself and everyone whom he draws into the project. *The Spire* also illuminates Golding's concern with a central confessional theme. He is trying to build his spire atop a church without foundations, crying that "God will provide" the necessary strength; the result indicates that God cannot provide man with his foundations and that man, like the Underground Man and all his successors, must seek those foundations within the self.

17. From a letter from Golding to John Peter, which Peter affixed to an essay when it was reprinted in William Nelson, ed., *William Golding's Lord of the Flies: A Source Book* (New York, Odyssey, 1963).

tial difference between the views of regeneration in *Darkness at Noon* and *Free Fall*. Both novels offer vivid illustrations of disintegration in the modern world, and both Rubashov and Sammy Mountjoy finally achieve blazing moments of perception. For Rubashov, however, perception can be only a mystical hope, unattainable for mankind until "later, much later" and beyond the reach of the hero himself, who is about to be executed. On the other hand, Sammy Mountjoy sees "God" in the midst of hell and plunges away from his religious perception back into life.

Koestler's hero, his life's system destroyed, turns at last to a religious vision; Golding takes the next step toward a reconstruction of values and applies his hero's religious perception to a reexamination of life. In such a reexamination, the pentecostal brilliance is dimmed by the reality of sin and weakness, but it is never extinguished. Although Sammy is denied the last bridge that would complete his pattern, Golding affirms the possibility that such a bridge can exist in the world, that the effort to reconstruct a pattern is indeed worthwhile. Such a pattern is rare (like "the taste of potatoes, element so rare that isotope of uranium is abundant by comparison"), and it is elusive, for it can be lost forever in one act. But it does exist, like a religious goal, heralded by a "flake of fire" and forever compelling modern man to sincere and passionate self-scrutiny.

4. THE FULL PERCEPTION:

Bellow

Ever since the Underground Man's initial statement of "over-acute consciousness," the modern confessional hero has sought a state of perception which will make his consciousness less painful and more meaningful. The Underground Man and the hero of *The Fall* embrace accusing visions of a community of guilt in an effort to alleviate their personal suffering. The Sartrean hero finds a glimmer of hope in the idea that he may create something which lives on, uniting him with the future. In Dmitri Karamazov's "babe," Rubashov's "oceanic sense," and Sammy Mountjoy's "vital morality," Dostoevsky, Koestler, and Golding offer meaning to their heroes in momentary, mystical visions.

All of these perceptions reveal the hero's self in relation to something else. For Dmitri, that "something else" is "all the suffering babes"; for Antoine Roquentin, it is the people who might one day read his book; for Rubashov, "the infinite"; for Sammy Mountjoy, "individual man." In one sense, however, this kind of perception cannot fully satisfy the hero's need for order in a disintegrated world. Because of its dependence on some factor outside itself, it cannot establish complete peace within the hero's mind, and it therefore proves ambiguous or impermanent. Redemptive religious visions are invariably fleeting for the modern hero, as they quickly become clouded by realities like Rubashov's wasted life and Dmitri's trial. More modest hopes, such as Roquentin's planned novel, seem unlikely ever to become reality, and the darker visions either fail to ease the hero's pain (the Underground Man) or simultaneously deny his freedom (Jean-Baptiste Clamence and Koestler's Communists).

This brief consideration of the nature and limitations of perception in the modern confessional novel is a necessary prelude to an evaluation of Saul Bellow's achievement within the genre. For it is Moses Herzog, the hero of Bellow's most brilliantly realized confessional novel, who arrives at a unique kind of perception—one which is in relation to nothing and, at the same time, to everything. An examination of this seemingly paradoxical state and of how it is achieved provides an understanding of what may be the ultimate possibility for the modern confessional hero.

Herzog's perception relates to nothing, in that it is a simple, quiet decision to stop his confession, a signal that his internal storm has at last been calmed; it simultaneously relates to everything, in that it indicates a profound understanding of his past and present existence. It contains nothing in the form of a momentary vision or an affirmation of one special value, but its development includes glimpses of almost everything in man's intellectual repertory. Finally, it relates to nothing because, conceived in isolation, it affirms the joy of isolation; yet this isolation simultaneously connects Moses Herzog with everything—in his rare state, both his mind and the world are at peace.

The unique nature of this perception is revealed most strikingly in the fact that Moses Herzog is the only confessional hero who calmly and willingly concludes his own confession. Other modern confessions leave the reader with a vague, uneasy feeling resembling that of Michel's friends in *The Immoralist*—a feeling that there is more to be said. *Notes from the Underground* and *Nausea* are introduced by "editor's notes" stating that each is only a fragment of a much longer journal; the implication is clear that the narrators would never cease writing of their own accord. Camus and Koestler achieve similar effects by ending their novels with references to earlier moments in the hero's confession, suggesting that many unsolved problems remain. Clamence considers the possibility of a second chance to save the drowning girl, and Rubashov dreams, as the bullet strikes him, that he is just being arrested. Finally, Golding turns our attention back, not to one stage of the hero's confession, but to a reexamination of its entire meaning, by introducing the "Sphinx's riddle" of the final sentence of *Free Fall*.

Since confession is motivated by an inner compulsion to understand, this type of hesitant, ambiguous ending indicates that the hero is not entirely satisfied, and his compulsion still exists within him. In *Herzog,* the hero's thoughts are organized around innumerable letters, impulsive jottings addressed to both personal acquaintances and public figures, living and dead. These letters, rarely completed or mailed, are written "endlessly, fanatically," with the urgency inherent in confession. In the final lines of the novel, however, Herzog decides to stop writing them:

> He lay, looking at the mesh of the screen, pulled loose by vines, and listening to the steady scratching of Mrs. Tuttle's broom. He wanted to tell her to sprinkle the floor. She was raising too much dust. In a few minutes he would call down

to her, "Damp it down, Mrs. Tuttle. There's water in the
sink." But not just yet. At this time he had no messages for
anyone. Nothing. Not a single word.[1]

The end to letter writing indicates the end of inner compulsion.
Herzog understands.

Before he arrives at this unprecedented level of peace and self-
understanding in his hero, Bellow considers many traditional
themes of the confessional genre. Two of these themes are developed to an extent which requires some discussion before we
can turn to a specific treatment of Bellow's work. First, the intellectual hero who has been developing throughout the course
of the confessional novel reaches a rich maturation in *Herzog;*
second, Bellow approaches the problem of suffering with the
sensitive insight of Jewish tradition.

"Your intelligence is so high," a friend tells Moses Herzog,
"—way off the continuum" (p. 43). Herzog employs his great
mental capacities not only as a thinker or philosopher in the sense
of the Sartrean hero, but also as a near-encyclopedic source of
intellectual references and allusions. He conveys much of the
"hum" which Sartre uses to portray the tormented mind—the
first line of the novel is "If I am out of my mind it's all right with
me"—and also manages to weave an elaborate web of parallel
images and phrases without losing any of the natural quality of
the language. It is one of the triumphs of *Herzog* that it is able
to encompass such a wide range of facts and thoughts without
becoming irrelevant or dull. The technique of having the hero
write letters to many scholarly colleagues gives some degree of
unity to his observations, but the manner in which they remain
consistently vital to his personal problems is chiefly attributable
to the remarkable use of irony.

1. Saul Bellow, *Herzog* (New York, Viking, 1964), p. 341. (Henceforth quotations from this novel will be identified by page numbers in
parentheses.)

In part, Bellow's irony resembles the satirical humor used so effectively by his modern Jewish counterparts, such as Salinger in "Franny" and Philip Roth in *Goodbye, Columbus*. It also includes an ironic view of the hero, undercutting his approaches to profundity in the manner of Dostoevsky and Sartre's use of the sharp letdown. This is apparent when Herzog takes a first casual step into confession:

> Resuming his self-examination, he admitted that he had been a bad husband—twice. . . . To his son and his daughter he was a loving but bad father. To his own parents he had been an ungrateful child. To his country, an indifferent citizen. To his brothers and his sister, affectionate and remote. With his friends, an egotist. With love, lazy. With brightness, dull. With power, passive. With his own soul, evasive. Satisfied with his own severity, positively enjoying the hardness and factual rigor of his judgment, he lay on his sofa, his arms rising behind him, his legs extended without aim.
>
> *But how charming we remain, notwithstanding.* (pp. 4–5)

Clearly, Bellow does not intend to let his hero off easily; Herzog's confession must be deep, sincere, unwaveringly relevant. Simple answers and bland generalizations will be exposed by the author's ironic comment, in a manner more direct, informal, and gently humorous than, but nevertheless reminiscent of, Camus in *The Fall*.

The most distinctive aspect of the irony in *Herzog* is not that of the author, but of the hero. He, too, can satirize others, as in his recollection of his wife's intellectual conversation with one of his colleagues: "From Soloviev, Mady naturally turned to Berdyaev, and while speaking of *Slavery and Freedom*—the concept of Sobornost—she opened the jar of pickled herring. Saliva spurted to Shapiro's lips" (p. 73). This satirical ability frequently adds life to basically gloomy scenes. As he undergoes a humiliat-

ing discussion with one of his wife's friends, he retains his capacity
to see the humor behind the social amenities. "I am not just another suburban hausfrau," claims the woman; Herzog emits the
desired response:

> "Well, I know you aren't like the other wives out here. . . ."
> Your kitchen is different, your Italian lamps, your carpets,
> your French provincial furniture, your Westinghouse, your
> mink, your country club, your cerebral palsy canisters are
> all different. (p. 38)

More important than his satiric wit, however, is Herzog's
capacity for self-directed irony. "There was a passionate satire in
him," and this quality is one of the basic tools of his self-scrutiny.
Just as the author undercuts the hero's own early attitude, Herzog
gradually comes to revel in an irreverent treatment of the generalizations which he and other intellectual historians had long
held dear. "Listen, Pulver!" he begins one letter to an austere
magazine editor who taught him at college. At other times, he
retreats from identification with scholarly conclusions into an
assumed naïveté: "Dear Doktor Professor Heidegger, I should
like to know what you mean by the expression 'the fall of the
quotidian.' When did this fall occur? Where were we standing
when it happened?" (p. 49) When his letters wander too far
from his examination of himself, Herzog frequently deflates his
own seriousness and reminds himself that the notes are not only
eccentric but presumptuous. When, in a letter to the *New York
Times,* he tries to maintain a pose of scholarly detachment, one
word shatters his act and directs his attention back to his own
life: *"Ours is a bourgeois civilization. I am not using this word in
a Marxian sense.* Chicken!" (p. 50) "I'm bugging all these
people," he thinks during one of his letters to public figures.
"Nehru, Churchill, and now Ike, whom I apparently want to give
a great books course" (p. 162). He sardonically justifies a message

133

to Spinoza—"He realized he was writing to the dead. To bring the shades of the great philosophers up to date" (p. 181)—and he concludes a lengthy tirade against one scholar's book: "Very good, Mermelstein. Go, and sin no more" (p. 318).

Herzog tends toward romantic notions, and these too are cut short by his own ironic sense. When he looks on his love affairs with half-serious, wide-eyed wonder—"What a lot of romances! One after another. Were those my real career?"—he counters with the memory of the mundane basis for his feeling toward his first wife Daisy and her mother: "Polina flew in . . . with a Quaker Oats box filled with apple strudel for Herzog. . . . It was extraordinary how much sensuality went into her baking. And she never gave Daisy the recipe" (p. 167). Similarly, his recollections of Sono, the Japanese mistress who did so much for his opinion of himself ("O mon philosophe, mon professeur d'amour"), fade from pride into whimsy. He remembers the baths she gave him: "I wonder who's scrubbing her now" (p. 173).

This, then, is Herzog's method of relating "the story of my life—how I rose from humble origins to complete disaster" (p. 152). Through his enduring irony, he maintains control over his wide-ranging thoughts, never allowing his intellectualism to separate him from his most pressing problems. In fact, his intellectual comments become an integral part of his mind, reflecting its whims as well as its suffering. Eventually, they lead him, in a gradual and painful progression, toward a harmonious relation of his mind with the world.

Bellow's success in handling Herzog's intellectualism can be seen more clearly in comparison with the less successful treatment of the subject in his first novel, *Dangling Man.* Early in that novel, the hero describes an incident in which he has gained some self-awareness. "I was leafing through Goethe's *Poetry and Life,*" he begins; then he tells of his reaction to the work, finally placing an example used by Goethe "beside that murderer Barnardine in *Measure for Measure.*" He concludes, "To be so drawn to those two was proof that I had indeed changed."[2] In this case, the intellectual sources approach the hero from without. He considers them and then relates their meaning to his life. His reading is, as his own term indicates, no more than an incident; it reveals no more or less than would any other action by the hero, and it begins and ends within well-defined limits. This is in sharp contrast to the intellectual flights of Herzog, relating historical figures in striking comparisons ("Governor Stevenson, I am sure the Coriolanus bit was painful"), seeing Nietzsche in his second wife Madeleine, and interrupting his most serious theories with memories from his own past, only to return to the theories in mid-sentence. The thoughts do not approach Herzog from the outside; they are within him, under his control but ready to burst forth whenever he relaxes his guard, and challenging him to find a true means of restoring order to his mind.

Father Herzog liked to repeat to his children the story of his painful existence. "We had a great schooling in grief," Moses recalls. The Jewish legacy of suffering is an important theme of *Herzog,* and it is interesting to note its special nature. The Jewish hero is not, like the Underground Man, "passionately in love with suffering"; he cannot share the malignant pleasure which Dostoevsky's hero finds in his humiliation and pain. However, he accepts suffering as his inevitable fate, and he takes a certain pride in knowing how to suffer. The Jew doesn't "love" suffering, but in a sense he needs it to feel his identity. To an outsider like the girl Ramona, this willingness to suffer appears masochistic. Similarly, Frank Alpine, whose slow transformation from anti-Semitic gentile into circumcised Jew is the central theme of Bernard Malamud's *The Assistant,* is bitterly exasperated by his friend Morris Bober's passive acceptance of pain: "That's what they live for, Frank thought, to suffer. And the one that has got

2. Saul Bellow, *Dangling Man* (Cleveland, Meridian, 1960), pp. 18–19. (Henceforth quotations from this novel will be identified by page numbers in parentheses.)

the biggest pain in the gut and can hold onto it the longest without running to the toilet is the best Jew. No wonder they got on his nerves."[3] When Frank approaches old Bober with his feelings, the grocer's answer expresses the Jewish pride in the tradition of suffering:

> "Tell me why it is that Jews suffer so damn much, Morris? It seems to me they like to suffer, don't they?"
> "Do you like to suffer? They suffer because they are Jews."
> "That's what I mean, they suffer more than they have to."
> "If you live, you suffer. Some people suffer more, but not because they want. But I think if a Jew doesn't suffer for the Law, he will suffer for nothing."[4]

Moses Herzog also has his law of suffering, and several times he reprimands himself for "suffering without proper dignity." His brutal friend Sandor Himmelstein is right when he calls Herzog "a real, genuine old Jewish type that digs the emotions" (p. 84). He "digs" them so much that his most carefree moments end in restatements of his need to suffer. Kissing the voluptuous Ramona at nine in the morning on Lexington Avenue, he wonders, "Was this perhaps the way to live? Had he had trouble enough, and paid his debt to suffering?" (p. 206) In that moment, "he had a taste of the life he might have led if he had been simply a loving creature. But as soon as he was alone in the rattling cab, he was again the inescapable Moses Elkanah Herzog." This commitment to suffering is also stated in his note to Sono:

> *I never had it so good,* he wrote. *But I lacked the strength of character to bear such joy.* That was hardly a joke. When a man's breast feels like a cage from which all dark birds have flown—he is free, he is light. And he longs to have his vultures back again. He wants his customary struggles, his

3. Bernard Malamud, *The Assistant* (New York, Signet, 1964), p. 71.
4. Ibid., p. 99.

nameless, empty works, his anger, his afflictions and his sins. (p. 169)

This is the testament of "foolish, feeling, suffering Herzog," the explanation of his strange acceptance of Madeleine's tyranny: "It would not be practical for her to hate herself. Luckily, God sends a substitute, a husband" (p. 174).

Bellow qualifies the theme of his hero's Jewish heritage in two important ways. First, the same element of irony which directs Herzog's intellectual excursions has a similar effect on references to his race. Herzog speaks of his ancestors in short phrases which remind us that he is a member of a suffering race, without attempting to blame any of his personal suffering on that race. Perhaps the finest example of this rueful humor is his lament about Madeleine: "She's built a wall of Russian books around herself. Vladimir of Kiev, Tikhon Zadonsky. In my bed! It's not enough they persecuted my ancestors!" (p. 59)

Bellow's second modification of the Jewish theme occurs in its relation to the novel as a whole. The serious writer faces a choice of two directions in which he can develop this theme. Malamud chooses what one critic aptly describes as "a moral and dramatic perspective which acknowledges no certainties except the fact of suffering."[5] In the tormented little world of the Bobers' tomb-like store, even the most well-meaning acts only increase the pain of the characters. Morris contracts fatal double pneumonia while shoveling snow on Sunday "for the goyim that they go to church"; Frank Alpine saves Helen Bober from a rapist, then turns her appreciation into hatred by forcing himself on her; at the funeral, Frank ventures too close to Bober's grave and falls in—an action which not only symbolizes his attraction to Bober's suffering, but also ruins the family's last pitiful approach to ceremonial dignity. In this world, the ultimate act which the hero can perform is his

5. Ihab Hassan, *Radical Innocence: Studies in the Contemporary American Novel* (Princeton, N.J., Princeton University Press, 1961), p. 166.

circumcision, his initiation into a full sharing of the suffering of the Jews. For Bellow, however, suffering is not the "only certainty." Herzog's ultimate act is not one of submission to pain but one of transcendence. Suffering presses upon him, and he accepts it; yet he also refuses to become immersed in it. His Jewish background is intrinsically related to his suffering, but the two are not synonymous. While Malamud's hero can fulfill his destiny only by embracing Jewish tradition, the creations of Bellow seem intent on escaping the bounds of that tradition—just as they seek to escape all the limitations on their existence.

The essential point is that, for Bellow, Jewish tradition is meant to define, not to determine; it is important only as long as it elucidates the nature of an individual's problem. Emphasizing his rejection of any Jewish "mystique" which would obscure the more universal aspects of the hero's problem, Bellow once remarked: "For us the pain of Shylock may be greater than for others because we are Jews, but it has fundamentally the same meaning" found in the pain of Job or Lear.[6] The idea of the individual throwing off all traditional modes is vividly expressed in *The Adventures of Augie March,* when the hero considers the rich Mrs. Renling's plan to adopt him: "There was a little in it of Moses and the Pharaoh's daughter; only I wasn't a bulrush-hidden infant by any means. I had family enough to suit me and history to be loyal to, not as though I had been gotten off a stockpile."[7] Just as the Underground Man would not be reconciled to the "wall" of reason and Raskolnikov destroyed himself in an effort to find an identity amid the terrible anonymity of St. Petersburg, Bellow's heroes will not be placed on a stockpile. They never cease to affirm their individual natures, and they accept their suffering, as well as their joy, as an intensely personal fact.

6. Ibid., p. 294. (Hassan quotes a remark made by Bellow in "The Jewish Writer and the English Literary Tradition," *Commentary* [October 1949], p. 366.)

7. Saul Bellow, *The Adventures of Augie March* (Greenwich, Conn., Crest, 1965), p. 160.

The Jewish theme, as applied to Herzog, introduces two central aspects of his confession. He is, on the one hand, an outcast, a descendant of the Wandering Jew; at the same time, he is deprived of the cultural continuity which sustains the Jews—he cannot hope for his child to achieve the peace which he himself has been denied, because that child has been snatched from him. As a Jew, Herzog is left out of the "oceanic visions of that sinister kraut," Spengler; he grows "sick with rage" as he reads, early in his life, "that I, a Jew, was born Magian and that we Magians had already had our great age, forever past. No matter how hard I tried, I would never grasp the Christian and Faustian world idea, forever alien to me" (p. 234). The bitter words leave him "infected with ambition" and compel him on in his later study of intellectual history, in a search for new "visions" which will include him. By the time of his confession, however, he has written only one book; "the rest of his ambitious projects had dried up, one after another" (p. 4). The essential solution to his alienation must be sought far from the "oceanic" realm, in his own personal world.

This idea is expressed in a characteristically ironic passage, in which Herzog realizes that he has finally been cast out—not only from his family and from this Faustian age but from the intellectual world through which he sought reentry: "Madeleine, by the way, lured me out of the learned world, got in herself, slammed the door, and is still in there, gossiping about me" (p. 77). His dislocation reaches its height in one memorable image. Lying in a West Side apartment with the Japanese girl Sono, amid her motley collection of Fourteenth Street bargain furniture (which includes "the broken Morris chair from the Catholic Salvage"), and conversing in "Yiddish French," Herzog is overwhelmed with his consummate failure to find a place in the world:

Is this really possible? Have all the traditions, passions, renunciations, virtues, gems, and masterpieces of Hebrew discipline and all the rest of it—rhetoric, a lot of it, but containing true facts—brought me to these untidy green sheets, and this rippled mattress? . . . The Jews were strange to the world . . . now the world is being strange to them in return. (p. 170)

In a striking ironic twist, the frustrations caused in Herzog's boyhood by the fact that he is Jewish have now been transformed into a deeper pain—the knowledge that he has lost the security of his Jewish heritage: "The more he thought, the worse his vision of the past" (p. 235). He has abandoned the religion of his ancestors, and he must suffer for it.

Out of the chaos of his disintegrated state, Herzog grasps at one messianic value, one "real matter . . . a reality" through which he might regain his "lost bearings." He plunges passionately on in search of her—"June. Out of cowardice, sickness, fraud, by a bungling father out of a plotting bitch, something genuine! This little daughter of his!" (p. 254) Yet at the moment when he finally accepts the loss of June, Herzog sees his own guilt. He has brought disinheritance on himself by rejecting his mother's religion: "Much heartbreak to relinquish this daughter. To become another lustful she-ass? Or a melancholy beauty like Sarah Herzog, destined to bear children ignorant of her soul and her soul's God?" (p. 274) There is an interesting aspect of this theme of disinheritance which further illuminates the author's treatment of Jewish themes. The disintegration of the messianic hope—and the craving to find some alternative—is crucial to the archetypal twentieth-century Jew, Joyce's Leopold Bloom. Bloom's plight is strikingly presented in archaic language which bridges the temporal gap back to its origins:

and now sir Leopold that had of his body no manchild for an heir looked upon him his friend's son and was shut up in sorrow for his forepassed happiness and as sad as he was that him failed a son of such gentle courage (for all ac-

counted him of real parts) so grieved he also in no less measure for young Stephen for that he lived riotously with those
wastrels and murdered his goods with whores.[8]

Again, Malamud and Bellow provide contrasting adaptations
of this typically Jewish theme. Morris Bober dreams constantly of
his dead son Ephraim and steadfastly refuses to consider the
gentile Frank as a kind of substitute; to Bober, Bloom's feelings
toward Stephen Dedalus would be incomprehensible. Herzog, on
the other hand, is seeking a satisfaction which is more psychological than racial or religious. This helps to explain his striking break
with tradition in desiring his daughter more than his son Marco;
he is not concerned with an heir who will carry on his name and
ideals, but with a meaningful reflection, however fleeting it may
prove, of his deepest feelings. "How well kids understand what
love is!" he thinks. "Marco was entering an age of silence and
restraint with his father, but Junie was exactly as Marco had
been." Ironically, this admission of how fast children change
indicates that his joyful vision of Junie is ultimately as devoid of
any hope of true stability as Bober's dream of his lost son.

While Bellow sought to apply the significant new insights of
the modern Jewish writer to the confessional novel, he remained
very much aware of his heritage from earlier confessional writers.
His first introspective hero, Joseph in *Dangling Man* (1944), is
in many ways a modern reproduction of the self-tortured and
rebellious Underground Man. The beginning of Joseph's journal
recalls the Underground Man's scornful rejection of the deter-
ministic, self-satisfied world around him:

> This is an era of hardboiled-dom. Today, the code of the
> athlete, of the tough boy . . . is stronger than ever. Do you
> have feelings? There are correct and incorrect ways of in-

8. James Joyce, *Ulysses* (New York, Modern Library, 1961), pp.
390–91.

dicating them. Do you have an inner life? It is nobody's business but your own. Do you have emotions? Strangle them. . . . Most serious matters are closed to the hardboiled. They are unpracticed in introspection, and therefore badly equipped to deal with opponents whom they cannot shoot like big game or outdo in daring.

If you have difficulties, grapple with them silently, goes one of their commandments. To hell with that! I intend to talk about mine. . . . In my present state of demoralization, it has become necessary for me to keep a journal—that is, to talk to myself. (p. 9)

Bellow's hero also exhibits the acute underground sense of self-humiliation. A rooming-house maid casually smokes in front of him because "she realizes I am of no importance," and he languishes in the pain of sitting at home while his wife supports him. He even causes an embarrassing scene in a restaurant by forcing himself on a contemptuous former acquaintance in a striking re-enactment of the Underground Man's compulsive approach to Zverkov and his former school friends. "I despise him . . . I'm going to go up to him and say hello whether he likes it or not. . . . Do you think I care about *him?*" shouts Joseph. "It's the principle . . . I have a right to be spoken to. I insist on it" (p. 33). This self-flagellation culminates in a repetition of the memorable underground contention that all men need suffering: "Trouble, like physical pain, makes us actively aware that we are living, and when there is little in the life we lead to hold and draw and stir us, we seek and cherish it, preferring embarrassment or pain to indifference" (p. 82).

In spite of these Dostoevskian echoes, however, Joseph is a very different kind of hero; the contrast between these two figures is suggested in the very titles of their confessions. The underground, however dark and grotesque it may be, offers an entrenchment, a solid base for the rebellious stance of that hero.

Joseph, on the other hand, can only dangle between the civilian and military worlds in a precarious freedom, unable to grasp any stable value. His existence is less akin to the Underground Man with his impassioned commitment to free will than it is to the illusory *dégagement* of Sartre's *Nausea;* for Joseph, life loses its meaning in "the derangement of days, the leveling of occasions."

As he tries to give coherence to his freedom, Joseph approaches several characteristic confessional visions. He turns on the reader, asking, "Was anyone immune? There were so many treasons." He considers the possibility of a meaningful "human community" and then of other "ideal constructions . . . each proclaiming: 'This is the only possible way to meet chaos' " (p. 140). Joseph even has his own demonic double, the "Spirit of Alternatives," who, like Ivan Karamazov's visitor, taunts him about the emptiness of his constructions and about his failure to find real meaning in his own freedom.

Through much of his journal, Joseph, waiting for the military call which has been endlessly delayed, refuses to get another job to replace the one he left, saying "I am unwilling to admit that I do not know how to use my freedom." Finally, after a series of petty and degrading clashes with the people around him, he admits defeat and rushes toward "the leash" of the army. This conclusion departs radically from the confessional idea of the self that clings to its identity in the face of all suffering and degradation. It represents the bleakest of modern visions, and Joseph's final cry, "Long live regimentation!" is as disturbing as the last line of this century's prototypical horror story, *1984:* "He loved Big Brother."[9]

In *Dangling Man,* Bellow brings the confessional novel into direct conflict with modern man's most negative view of freedom; the result seriously questions the validity of self-knowledge in this

9. George Orwell, *1984* (New York, Signet, 1961), p. 245.

143

chaotic era. If this novel were the author's only approach to confessional writing, it would remain interesting but ultimately disappointing. Bellow's style has not yet come alive and reflects the hero's colorless and slow-paced life in accurate but uncompelling ways. As we have mentioned, he has yet to make his intellectual references an organic part of the narrative. And finally, although he has defined the rebellious instinct in the modern hero, Bellow has not yet found the channel through which that spirit might flow toward a full and significant perception of the self and the world.

His next novel, *The Victim* (1947), brings a Jew and an anti-Semite into a clash in which roles are perverted and both men inflict increasing pain on themselves. It constitutes an important step in Bellow's transformation of the Jewish "motif" into a Jewish "theme" which is personally relevant to the hero. Furthermore, it is an interesting application of the technique of the double. It is not, however, until his third novel, *The Adventures of Augie March* (1953), that the author escapes the stylistic limitations of his dark studies and creates a completely satisfying work.

Augie March and Bellow's other broad picaresque novel, *Henderson the Rain King* (1958), both deserve extensive comment, but we will limit ourselves to mention of a few of the factors in them which point toward the author's eventual return to the confessional form in *Herzog.* Augie is the classic quixotic hero, whose innocence lights even his most sordid experiences and alleviates the gloom that hangs over Bellow's earlier novels. By the final line of this far-ranging narrative, the hero can affirm "the *animal ridens* in me, the laughing creature forever rising up."[10] Tempered by suffering and bitter experience, this spirit will nevertheless remain in Moses Herzog as one source of the indomitable irony which modulates and controls his confession. Henderson, Bellow's only Gentile hero, is disinherited from his

10. Bellow, *Augie March,* p. 556.

family and seeks his own peace through external action on a grand scale. In the end, all his wild adventures lead to an internal vision of wisdom and love which makes the novel "the most affirmative of Bellow's works"[11] up to that point and offers, in its external way, the hopeful possibility of a progression from disintegration into meaning.

Bellow's most brilliant early portrayal of the disintegration with which Herzog would be confronted is in the short novel *Seize the Day* (1956). Tommy Wilhelm, a failure in life, is in his forties, living in a West Side New York hotel under the premature shadow of death. Surrounded by old people, he is constantly aware that his own existence is slipping away from him and seeks desperately to grasp some stable object in the world. He is separated from his wife, who will not even grant him the freedom of a divorce, preferring to bleed him persistently for the support of their two children. Finally, Wilhelm is irrevocably cut off from his own heritage. He repudiated his father early in life in order to pursue the American Dream in Hollywood; the crowning indignity of his ungratefulness consisted in changing his name. His old father, Doctor Adler, still calls him "Wilky" and stings him every time he tells friends, "My son and I use different monickers. I uphold tradition. He's for the new."[12]

For Tommy Wilhelm, the price of being "for the new" is bitter humiliation and suffering. His wife keeps him broke, and his wealthy father gently but firmly refuses all his tortured, self-abasing requests for help. At the height of his misfortune, he places all his faith in a swindler named Dr. Tamkin, who lures him with a promise not only of riches but of meaning within the terrifying flux of Tommy's world. Overcome by his bleak past and hopeless future, Tommy follows Tamkin into the uptown commodities market to "Seize the day." Here Bellow carries Wilhelm's disintegration to its darkest extreme. The old men of

11. Hassan, p. 321.
12. Saul Bellow, *Seize the Day* (New York, Viking, 1961), p. 14.

the hotel are replaced by the ghostly near-blind Rappaport; what money Tommy had left is lost; and he only confirms his father's opinion that he is a hopeless sucker. Out of all this, however, there emerges a hint that regeneration is possible—although it remains far from the hero's reach.

At one point Wilhelm bemoans his inability to communicate with anyone amid the "complexity and machinery" of New York:

> You had to translate and translate, explain and explain, back and forth, and it was the punishment of hell itself not to understand or be understood, not to know the crazy from the sane, the wise from the fools, the young from the old or the sick from the well. The fathers were no fathers and the sons no sons. You had to talk with yourself in the daytime and reason with yourself at night. Who else was there to talk to?[13]

Tommy is never quite capable of following the prescription for confession which he implies in this thought. He is inevitably sidetracked by his self-pity or concern with material problems. The only real hope offered in *Seize the Day* is the solemn but ambiguous final scene. Ushered by mistake into a stranger's wake, the hero suddenly feels a deep communion with the dead man— and perhaps with all men at the nadir of disintegration. Enveloped in the funeral music, he "sank deeper than sorrow, through torn sobs and cries toward the consummation of his heart's ultimate need."[14]

Critics have found every emotion from self-pity to visionary love in Tommy Wilhelm's moving tears.[15] One valuable approach to their meaning might be a comparison with the tears

13. Ibid., p. 84.
14. Ibid., p. 118.
15. Hassan sees the most hopeful sign in Wilhelm's tears—a "consummation of love" bringing "piercing insight and release" (p. 314). He also mentions that other critics have seen this climax as a nadir of self-pity.

146

shed by Sammy Mountjoy in the prison cell of *Free Fall*. Sammy's cry was at once both the lowest instinctive action to which the disintegrated human being can sink and the moment of purgation. He emerges with tears still on his face, stripped of all superficial systems and concerns, to confront the full reality of his existence. Wilhelm's sobs also mark the lowest point of his humiliation and decline; perhaps he too can come forth, free of his superficial worries about money and age, and achieve self-knowledge. This vague possibility—as far from being a "vision" as it is from self-pity—looks ahead to the hero who will finally make it real, the hero "overcome by the need to explain, to have it out, to justify, to put in perspective, to clarify, to make amends,"[16] in short, the hero of *Herzog*.

Darkness at Noon, in which the hero frequently compares himself to Moses, and *Free Fall,* with its relation to the Fall from Paradise, suggest that the confessional hero's quest for reconstructed values leads him toward mythic patterns. In *Herzog,* Bellow brings modern man even closer to myth. The hero's life is the quest of a modern Moses for his own Promised Land. Herzog seeks fulfillment by leading his wife Madeleine and his friends Valentine and Phoebe Gersbach to the peaceful country life of Ludeyville. His flock soon deserts him, and his quest proves disastrous. Left alone, he sees himself as "a broken-down monarch of some kind." His confession is a renewal of his search, a pilgrimage through his disintegrated life toward a state of true peace and perception. The theme of this mental journey remains linked to the story of Moses, but its structure of rambling meditations and memories is organized on the pattern of the *Odyssey*.

When he begins his first search, Moses Herzog is married to a woman named Daisy. "Stability, symmetry, order, containment were Daisy's strength," he recalls. "By my irregularity and tur-

16. Bellow, *Herzog,* p. 2. (Cited by note to avoid ambiguity, because it is mentioned in context of discussion of *Seize the Day*.)

bulence of spirit I brought out the very worst in Daisy" (p. 126). In seeking a life more attuned to his own spirit, Herzog is attracted to a woman even more unpredictable and passionate than himself. His relationship with Madeleine is described as a constant, raging battle, in which he proves hopelessly overmatched. The nature of their struggle is elucidated by the symbols which come to represent their battle standards. Moses, reading Blake's poems, marks his place with "the slip of paper on which Edvig had listed the traits of paranoia" (p. 80). In her Catholic days, Madeleine "read all the gossip columnists. Her bookmarks in St. Augustine and in her missal were clippings from the *Post* and *Mirror*" (p. 115). While he can barely hold his intellectual power within the bounds of sanity, she is trying to embrace everything in the world at once. These bookmarks are a striking illustration of the truth of Herzog's admission that "there was a flavor of subjugation in my love for Madeleine" (p. 8).

Madeleine Herzog is one of the most memorable women to appear in a confessional novel, a radical departure from such passive and pliable reflections of the hero as Dostoevsky's holy prostitutes, Marceline in *The Immoralist,* Arlova in *Darkness at Noon,* and Beatrice Ifor in *Free Fall.* In her claim that she is "going through a long crisis" and "rethinking everything," Madeleine recalls Anny in Sartre's *Nausea,* struggling with the inadequacy of the "perfect moments" on which she had tried to build her existence. In their intellectual crises, both these women extend their roles as mirrors by offering more complete reflections of the minds of the heroes. But Madeleine is a much more fully developed individual than Anny. The only woman in this study with whom she can really be compared is Grushenka in *The Brothers Karamazov.* With their wild, impetuous natures, their pride, and their vast power over men, Madeleine and Grushenka reflect aspects of the heroes' personalities; but they also exert tremendous power over them and lead Herzog and Dmitri toward destruction.

Madeleine is a fascinating psychological study in her own right. Her past has been a "grotesque nightmare" which has produced such a tumultuous mixture of hatreds and passions within her that Moses, struggling to maintain his own balance, can still describe her as paranoid. Madeleine's father has betrayed his wife and maltreated his daughter, causing her to distrust all men, as well as the Jewish religion in which she was brought up. Her beauty enables her to translate her resentments into a bitter and triumphant pride, and she taunts Moses: "Still young . . . young, beautiful, full of life. Why should I waste it all on you" (p. 21). Her strange and intense craving for power is lucidly portrayed during her conversion to Catholicism, when she leads Herzog to conclude, "Difficulty was the whole object. She wanted Moses and the Monsignor to struggle over her" (p. 115). And she possesses the ability to satisfy this craving, as Herzog admits during a conversation with one of her friends: "Madeleine had convinced Zelda that she too was exceptional. Everyone close to Madeleine, everyone drawn into the drama of her life became exceptional, deeply gifted, brilliant. It had happened to him also" (p. 38).

Madeleine gradually destroys Moses' control over his life and reduces all its order to chaos. He has been drifting away from his Jewish heritage all his life, as he realized during his affair with the Japanese girl Sono; but Madeleine forces him to reject it outright in a painful ritual of surrender. He begins to feel this pain when she makes him accompany her to church: "He was a husband, a father. He was married, he was a Jew. Why was he in church?" He proceeds to give up his first wife and son, but she insists on extracting the final toll. His submission emphasizes his growing helplessness and humility:

"Maybe I have become a fanatic about conventional things," said Madeleine. "But I won't have it any other way. You and I have got to marry in the Church, otherwise I quit. Our children will be baptized and brought up in the Church."

149

> Moses gave a dumb half-nod. Compared with her he felt
> static, without a temperament. ((pp. 116–17)

In a gesture of total renunciation of his past, Moses invests all
his father's savings, "representing forty years of misery in America," in the Ludeyville house and spends a year rebuilding it as
the site of his Promised Land. Madeleine reacts by keeping it in
constant disorder. Herzog makes several attempts to reassert his
own position with her. Before they marry, he takes some pleasure
in the fact that "She had been a Catholic for only three months,
and already because of Herzog she couldn't be confessed, not by
Monsignor, anyway" (p. 112). But this victory fades quickly,
and, by making him feel like a corruptor, Madeleine humbles
Herzog still more. At Ludeyville, he tries again to gain the upper
hand by requiring her to make love on the bathroom floor; this
desperate effort only feeds her constant interior rage. When
Herzog, still possessing his powerful intellect, first clashes directly
with Madeleine concerning his disordered house, the result is one
of the most unforgettable scenes in the novel; it is worth quoting
at length as a brilliant example of Madeleine's terrifying power:

> Madeleine said quickly, firmly, and accurately, "You'll never
> get the surroundings *you* want. Those are in the twelfth cen-
> tury somewhere. . . . Okay—let's hear your old sad story.
> Tell me about your poor mother. . . . Oh, what balls!"
> "As if you didn't have a past of your own."
> "Oh, balls! So now we're going to hear how you SAVED me.
> . . . You SAVED me. You SACRIFICED your freedom. I
> took you away from Daisy and your son, and your Japanese
> screw. Your important time and money and attention." Her
> wild blue glare was so intense that her eyes seemed twisted.
> "Madeleine!"
> "Oh—shit!"
> "Just think a minute."

"What do you know about thinking?"

"Maybe I married you to improve my mind," said Herzog. "I'm learning."

"Well, I'll teach you, don't worry!" said the beautiful, pregnant Madeleine between her teeth. (p. 124–25)

This exchange ends like a clap of doom, an ominous declaration that Madeleine will always be in control of both Herzog and the child, June, who is still within her.

Madeleine proceeds to rob Herzog of all his friends, systematically demolishing the foundations on which his existence rests. With her increasing scholarly interests, she dominates Moses' colleague Shapiro when he visits them; with her wild emotions, she even gains control of their psychiatrist, Edvig; and she uses Herzog's old friend Sandor Himmelstein as her lawyer when she files for divorce. Most important, she takes away his best friend, Valentine Gersbach, whom Moses brought with them to the country to complement the anticipated joys of his Promised Land. She and Gersbach add the final injury by convincing Moses to pay a year's rent on a Chicago house, just before they evict him from it.

Betrayed on all sides, Herzog is not unwilling to accept some of the blame. He at last sees that his approach to peace was a gesture of pride, doomed to the collapse which inevitably faces a construction that is too far above reality:

When I think of Valentine . . . I see the mobs breaking into the palaces and churches and sacking Versailles, wallowing in cream desserts or pouring wine over their dicks and dressing in purple velvet, snatching crowns and miters and crosses. (p. 215)

Madeleine and Valentine have indeed broken into his "palace." She dons his intellectual cloak and Gersbach replaces Moses as a

Chicago personality and, most cruelly, as Junie's father. Nothing remains that is Herzog's own.

In this state of disorder and despair, the hero begins his second quest for a meaningful life. His confession, which continues for five days, covers a wide range of memories and thoughts; many of these are fascinating in themselves, but they never lose the unity and coherence which is implied in their mythic organization. Moses Herzog's search for his Promised Land is a kind of mental epic, and Bellow, like Joyce, uses the *Odyssey* as the basis of his structure. Odyssean themes are neither as prominent nor as consciously invoked in *Herzog* as they are in *Ulysses,* and the hero's quest remains as close to that of Moses as it is to that of Odysseus. Nevertheless, this source provides an illuminating insight into the form and the overall significance of Herzog's vast and chaotic range of thoughts.

Herzog's confession can be divided into five movements, each distinguished by an external action. The first is a gesture of escape, an attempt to find meaning in exile; he takes a train from New York to Cape Cod for a vacation but returns the same night, unable to rest. His thoughts while he rides are a dirge of disintegration, an echo of another epic vision of modern man, Eliot's *The Waste Land*. The second phase is a night at home, during which Herzog listens to the song of the Sirens from his past. His glimpse at past romances brings a faint light into his world, but love is ultimately seen as elusive and destructive. In the third section, Herzog spends a night with Ramona—his Nausicaa— and considers her offer of peace and happiness. On the following day, the hero begins his journey through hell, which takes him to the New York criminal court and then to the origin of his sufferings in Chicago, outside the house occupied by Madeleine and Gersbach. Only after the purification of this episode can he proceed to the fifth stage of his confession, in which he returns to Ludeyville and finds true perception.

As Herzog prepares to board his train for Cape Cod, his view of the world is expressed in his newspaper, "a hostile broth of black print *Moonraceberlin-Khruschchwarncommitteegalactic-XrayPhouma"* (p. 34). He is willing to abandon his place in such a world and feels disappointed that a doctor has found him physically healthy: "He had been hoping for some definite illness which would send him to the hospital for a while. He would not have to look after himself" (p. 13). In this state of mind, he reminds us of the depraved hero of Camus' *The Fall:* "Madeleine refused to be married to him, and people's wishes have to be respected. Slavery is dead" (p. 70). All Herzog's letters and recollections during the train ride crystallize in the cry of Sandor Himmelstein: "We're all whores in this world, and don't you forget it." In his past, Moses finds only deceit. As he recalls carrying his friend Shapiro's book through Europe, his thoughts assume the images and rhythms of *The Waste Land:*[17]

> Herzog kept reading away at it for the sake of the discipline, and under a growing burden of guilt. Abed in Belgrade, at

17. Herzog's description of his fruitless journey particularly recalls ll. 209 ff. of Eliot's *The Waste Land:*
> Mr. Eugenides, the Smyrna merchant . . .
> Asked me in demotic French
> To luncheon at the Cannon Street Hotel
> Followed by a weekend at the Metropole.
> At the violet hour, when the eyes and back
> Turn upward from the desk, when the human engine waits
> Like a taxi throbbing waiting . . .

Two other striking similarities between *Herzog* and Eliot's poem might be mentioned. Moses' desperate search for help from Gersbach and Himmelstein recalls the helpless appeal of the women in "A Game of Chess" (ll. 113–15):
> "What are you thinking of? What thinking?
> "What?
> "I never know what you are thinking. Think."

Herzog also shares Eliot's negative view of regeneration. The opening lines of *The Waste Land* are echoed in Herzog's statement:
> Early in June, when the general revival of life troubles many people, the new roses, even in shop windows, reminding them of their own failures, of sterility and death, Herzog went to have a medical checkup (p. 12).

> the Metropol, with bottles of cherry juice, the trolley cars
> whizzing past in the frozen night. (p. 69)

Sandor's affirmation of universal whoredom, compounded by Moses' increasing consciousness of the "age of spiritual exhaustion" which he had first encountered in Spengler, suggests another important modern statement of disintegration. In *Ulysses,* during a discussion of Shakespeare, Stephen Dedalus mentions Ann Hathaway to his friend Eglinton:

> —She lies laid out in stark stiffness in that second-best bed, the mobled queen . . . Agenbite of inwit: remorse of conscience. It is an age of exhausted whoredom groping for its god.
> —History shows that to be true, *inquit Eglintonus Chronololologos.* The ages succeed one another. But we have it on high authority that a man's worst enemies shall be those of his house and family.[18]

This passage provides a fitting overture for Moses Herzog's first excursions into his past.

As the hero recalls a series of meetings with the friends who were quietly deserting him for Madeleine, Bellow presents an interesting variation of the technique of the double. This is shown most clearly in the treatment of Valentine Gersbach and Sandor Himmelstein. Both of these men to some extent resemble the hero —they are "good old-time Jews," schooled in suffering and quick to show their feelings. Like Madeleine, however, they are individuals, and their individuality negates their effectiveness as mirrors. In fact, they resemble each other far more than they do Herzog, and it is this fact that allows them to fulfill one function of some doubles—to heighten the hero's pain and suffering. Gersbach and Himmelstein both give Moses exactly the same advice; the repetition of their words—"It's your own frigging fault!"— infuses them with special significance for Herzog. He becomes

18. Joyce, *Ulysses,* p. 206.

so resigned to his humiliation that he even accepts Gersbach's command that he ignore the most painful fact of his situation and "knock it off, about the kid."

The ironic aspect of Herzog's confrontations with these two doubles is that, like Koestler's Rubashov during his interrogations, he sinks into humiliation through his own thoughts, which have little relevance to the accusations being made against him. Herzog is forced to admit his weakness, not by the words of Valentine and Sandor, but by his own awareness of their strength. "Dealing with Valentine was like dealing with a king," he says. "He might have held a scepter. He *was* a king, an emotional king, and the depth of his heart was his kingdom" (p. 61). With Sandor, he continues to see his helplessness, telling himself, "Very well, Moshe Herzog —if you must be pitiable, sue for aid and succor, you will always put yourself, inevitably, in the hands of these angry spirits" (p. 86).

Soon Herzog feels inferior to these men not only in emotions and power, but also in his self-declared "special province" of suffering. Gersbach, speaking "as a man who has risen from terrible defeat, the survivor of sufferings few could comprehend," retells his story of how he lost his leg. Sandor is deformed by a hunched back, inflicted at Normandy; this "made Herzog uneasy, perhaps, that he had been discharged from the Navy owing to asthma and never saw action" (p. 79). Sadly, Moses admits that he cannot even claim a deeper suffering than his tormentors:

> Moses recognized that under his own rules the man who had suffered more was more special, and he conceded willingly that Gersbach had suffered harder, that his agony under the wheels of the boxcar must have been far deeper than anything Moses had ever suffered. (p. 62)

In recalling the depths of humiliation to which his two doubles drive him, Herzog does not lose his own sense of irony. He remembers the "amorphous, swelling, hungry, indiscriminate, cowardly potato love" with which they softened their damning words, and he cries out within himself, "Oh, you sucker," as he

155

realizes that Gersbach and Sandor are as insecure and weak as himself. Sandor has been quick to excuse Madeleine for her messy house, but he himself flies into a wild rage when he finds dirty dishes in his sink. He tells Moses that he is seeing a psychiatrist and shouts, in an echo of the hero's own disinheritance, "They're killing me! Killing their father!" When he enlists Herzog to speak to his teen-aged daughter, Moses begins to see the shallowness of Himmelstein's advice: "It's all very well for me to surrender my daughter, but his little hamsters have to have elevating discourses" (p. 90).

Gersbach's wall of pretense and emotion is more difficult to penetrate, and Herzog still cannot escape all his humiliating feelings toward Valentine. During the train ride, however, he does assemble all the advice of Edvig, Valentine, and Sandor into a parody of religious insight, a bitter comment on the possibilities of trust and communication. These three men—the "calm Protestant Anglo-Celtic," analytical and alien, and the old Jewish pals with their outpourings of affection—all contribute to Herzog's mocking meditation on Martin Buber:

> By means of spiritual dialogue, the I-It relationship becomes an I-Thou relationship. God comes and goes in man's soul. And men come and go in each other's souls. Sometimes they come and go in each other's beds, too. You have dialogue with a man. You have intercourse with his wife. . . . You give him consolation. All the while you rearrange his life. You even make out his budget for years to come. You deprive him of his daughter. . . . And finally your suffering is greater than his, too, because you are the greater sinner. And so you've got him, coming and going. (p. 64)

These thoughts finally convince Herzog that his flight from his situation is useless; he sees escape as an admission of defeat which unites him only with "this gray-faced conductor, one of an ancient vanishing breed." Pursued by images of his disintegration, he cannot travel fast enough to elude them, yet he is moving too fast to grasp at peace or perception. "Well, what do you want?" he asks himself. "An angel from the skies? The train would run him over" (p. 66). By the time he arrives at the Vineyard, he knows "I never should have come." He fumbles through a few hours with his kind hosts, then slips out of the house and returns home the same night.

The next stage of Herzog's confession, the song of his Sirens, begins when he rereads the letter from Geraldine Portnoy which had initially forced him to accept the truth about Madeleine and Valentine. This letter is a brilliant transition, because it emphasizes the shift of focus from "friendships" to "romances" and simultaneously indicates the emptiness of the negative, ironic commentary which had characterized Moses' letters on the train. Geraldine, a bright and serious graduate student, anxious to be diplomatic and make a good impression on Professor Herzog, summons all her best scholarly jargon to her task. Her letter becomes an ironic pastiche of ideas which Herzog had thought were his own original and penetrating observations. His review of Shapiro's book—"too much imaginary history . . . clinical psychologists might write fascinating histories. Put professionals out of business" (p. 77)—is thrown back at him in Geraldine's sober warning: "My scientific background has taught me to make more cautious generalizations, and resist this creeping psychoanalysis of ordinary conduct" (p. 99). She also shows that his observation about Madeleine's effect on Zelda had not been particularly unique: "It is extremely exciting to talk with her, she gives a person a sense of the significant encounter—with life—a beautiful, brilliant person with a fate of her own" (p. 100).

Moses' awareness of his pretensions and errors, implied in Geraldine's letter, comes to a more dramatic realization as he recalls his proud plans for the book he was to write at Ludeyville:

> He was going—he smiled secretly now, admitting it—to wrap the subject up, to pull the carpet from under all the other scholars, to show them what was what, stun them,

157

expose their triviality once and for all. It was not simple vanity, but a sense of responsibility that was the underlying motive. (p. 119)

Now, however, he sees that nothing is so simple and attainable; confronted with his heightened awareness of disintegration, he wonders whether he would even want such a "sense of responsibility" any longer. After his scathing letter to the priest who converted Madeleine, he reflects:

Suppose that I am absolutely right and the Monsignor, for example, is absolutely wrong. If I am right, the problem of the world's coherence, and all responsibility for it, becomes mine. How will it make out when Moses E. Herzog has his way? No, why should I take that on myself? (p. 155)

Much of his consideration of the women of his past is naturally taken up with Madeleine. As he remembers his associations with her father and mother, as well as with the Monsignor, her strange character comes into clear focus. The turbulent and conflicting forces around her ultimately leave her untouched and impervious, an archetype of strength and constancy amid the wasteland which surrounds her:[19]

But when all was said and done, Madeleine didn't marry in the church, nor did she baptize her daughter. Catholicism went the way of zithers and tarot cards, bread-baking and Russian civilization. And life in the country. (p. 118)

Madeleine is followed by a parade of other women—the Polish girls Wanda and Zinka, his first wife Daisy, Sono, and Ramona, who interrupts his thoughts with her phone call. From these subjects he drifts into memories of childhood and his family. Many of his recollections are pleasant, but, in the end, Herzog always finds meaningful and lasting love impossible. The significance of

19. Madeleine is brought into *The Waste Land* through the tarot cards used by "Madame Sosotris, famous clairvoyante," in the poem.

this section is best illustrated by two polar examples of love—the pathetic Nachman and Sono, Herzog's delightful Japanese girl.

Nachman, a boyhood friend of the hero, is another of the "old-time Jews" who form a network of allusive doubles around Moses Herzog. "Lecturing in his unreal way," Nachman presents the extreme opposite of Sandor Himmelstein's cynicism and Gersbach's false displays of affection. His fervent, emotional love leaves him helpless in a world dominated by the Himmelsteins and Gersbachs, and his life slips away from him while he lies on a borrowed cot in a friend's apartment, paying homage, with his girl Laura, to the only truth he knows. "In our ecstasies we had to warn each other to be more moderate," he tells Herzog. "It was like a holy act—we mustn't make the gods jealous" (p. 133). This "unreal" life soon meets its inevitable end. Laura is last seen in an insane asylum, trying to slash her wrists, and Nachman runs away when he sees his old friend Herzog on the street. As Moses watches this comical and pathetic figure shuffling away from him on Eighth Street, he realizes that he himself has come, by a more circuitous route, to the same disastrous conclusion of love: "Perhaps, thought Herzog, the sight of *me* frightened *him*. Have I changed even more than he has?" The fact that Nachman will not speak to him also adds to his suffering by reminding him that he has denied himself all contact with even the most pitiful values of his childhood.

The more satisfying side of his past romances is represented by Sono, the Oriental beauty as enchanting as any Siren. But Sono's diverse furnishings and the "funny Yiddish French" in which they converse only emphasize the decay of his heritage and distract him from his image of the Promised Land. Like Odysseus, Herzog keeps his sights on his goal. Her lilting song to "mon Moso" draws him, resisting, to her room, and he recalls the struggles and temptations:

> He violently desired Sono, and just as violently did not want to go. Even now he felt the fever, remembered the

smells, experienced the difficulty. . . . Other men have forsaken the West, looking for just this. It was delivered to me
in New York City. (pp. 171–73)

Odysseus' description of his own trial is quite similar:

The lovely voices appealing in ardor over the water made me
crave to listen, and I tried to say 'Untie me!' to the crew,
jerking my brows; but they bent steady to the oars. . . .
So all rowed on, until the Seirenes dropped under the sea
rim, and their singing dwindled away.[20]

Sono's singing also dwindles into a final sad phrase, "Je souffre
trop." Moses has held his course; he begins to date Madeleine.

The love which Herzog recalls in his past comes to its full
realization in the present when he goes to see Ramona. Like
Odysseus' meeting with Nausicaa at the stream, the visit to Ramona begins with an act of washing. In her bathroom—"a lux-
urious little room with indirect lighting (kindness to haggard
faces)"—Moses cleanses himself of the "sea-brine" of his train
ride through decay and disintegration. He emerges into a reenactment of the banquet of Alcinous; while he eats her shrimp Arnaud
and sips chilled wine, he is encouraged to talk at length about his
"adventures" on the first disastrous journey toward his Promised
Land.

Ramona satisfies his sensuality, his need to confess, even his
desire to feel strong again. She offers her own kind of peace and
regeneration; but she is limited, and her solutions, however
pleasant, are ultimately as far from the goal of his confession as
Sono's delights were from the goal of his first pilgrimage. She
earns a high compliment from the hero who has known so many
false friends—"She was genuine"—but she lives in a completely
physical world in which pleasure can bring no lasting perception.

20. Homer, *The Odyssey,* trans. Robert Fitzgerald (Garden City, N.Y.,
Doubleday, 1961), p. 228 (Bk. 12, ll. 195–203).

She cannot fully understand Moses' deepest feelings, because she "does not believe in any sin but the sin against the body." Herzog finally admits her limitations in an ironic thought: "an injured heart, and raw gasoline poured on the nerves. And to this, what does Ramona answer? She says, get your health back. *Mens sana in corpore sano.* Constitutional tension of whatever origin needed sexual relief" (p. 201). When called upon for a more profound solution, Ramona can offer only a standard modern code of perseverance, a paean to the "hardboiled-dom" which Bellow first rejects in *Dangling Man* and which remains irrelevant to the central problem of Herzog:

> What he really must do, she went on, in the same operatic style . . . was to pay his debt for the great gifts he had received, his intelligence, his charm, his education, and free himself to pursue the meaning of life, not by disintegration, where he would never find it, but humbly and yet proudly continuing his learned studies. (p. 184)

Herzog's reaction to this is predictable—"He, Herzog, overtake life's meaning! He laughed into his hands, covering his face." In spite of her shortcomings, Herzog is more than willing to accept Ramona's attempts to "renew the spirit through the flesh"; skillful and voluptuous, she is exquisitely capable of bringing him a momentary joy. But what she views as a full regeneration—"with him she experienced a real Easter"—remains inadequate for Moses. Like Nausicaa, Ramona offers a land and shelter vastly preferable to the torments the hero has undergone, but it is only a pleasant stop on his journey toward a deeper peace.

On the way to Ramona's, Herzog hums a tune and tries, in a manner reminiscent of Roquentin's approach to meaning in *Nausea,* "to capture, as if it were an elusive fragile thread, the reason why these old songs were running through his head." Ramona cannot assist him in this effort; she obscures the old songs with her own favorite music, a harsh hymn to human resourcefulness. On her stereo set, "Mohammad el Bakkar kept singing his winding, nasal, insinuating songs to the sounds of wire coathangers moved back and forth, and drums, tambourines and mandolins and bagpipes" (p. 187). This combination of instruments from diverse cultures recalls the components of Sono's apartment and further accentuates the inadequacy of Ramona's world for Herzog. He does not resist her offerings or feel guilty in accepting them, as he did with Sono; but he maintains his awareness of their ludicrous aspects. One striking example of this occurs during the ritual cleansing in the bathroom, when he jolts himself sharply from solemnity to bawdy humor:

> He recalled the old Jewish ritual of nail water, and the word in the Haggadah, *Rachatz!* "Thou shalt wash." It was obligatory also to wash when you returned from the cemetery (*Beth Olam*—the Dwelling of the Multitude). But why think of cemeteries, of funerals now? Unless . . . the old joke about the Shakespearean actor in the brothel. When he took off his pants the whore in bed gave a whistle. He said, "Madam, we come to bury Caesar, not to praise him." (p. 181)

Ramona is a florist, and her apartment always resembles a garden, a fitting setting for the sensual paradise which she offers. Moses finds humor in this, too, musing, "There is a distant garden where curious objects grow, and there, in a lovely dusk of green, the heart of Moses E. Herzog hangs like a peach." This image leads him to sense his own clownish appearance, and he brings to Ramona's paradise an ironic comment on himself, his failure with Madeleine, and the inadequacy of his affair with Sono:

> He dried the sweatband of his straw hat. . . . And who wore such a hat, such a blazer? Why, Lou Holtz, of course, the old vaudeville comic. He sang, "I picked a lemon in the garden of life, where only *peaches* grow." Herzog's face

again quickened with a smile. The old Oriental Theatre in Chicago. Three hours of entertainment for two bits. (p. 175)

Moses' irony seems to leave him later in the evening, as he nears the fulfillment of Ramona's monumental sensual promise. Waiting for her in bed, he wonders whether he should accept her solution, which, for all its faults, does offer a substitute for one of the most burning voids in his life: "He could be a patriarch, as every Herzog was meant to be. The family man, father, trans-mitter of life" (p. 202). On this note, he begins his beautiful, peaceful night with Ramona, from which they emerge into the bright and promising morning. After the long kiss on Lexington Avenue, however, he climbs into the cab and his joy fades back into irony. He resumes his journey.

Moses Herzog's trip through hell is the longest of the five sec-tions of his confession, a wandering adventure which takes him from New York to Chicago and forces his consciousness into the depths of his intellectual and spiritual existence. It begins with a call to the lawyer Simkin and the thought, "I should have phoned Simkin earlier." This casual phrase suggests that Herzog has been in need of some positive gesture for some time and reminds us that he had indeed attempted a kind of journey to hell before. That first effort was the trip to Europe which Moses took just before the beginning of his confession. *"This year I covered half the world,"* he writes to the Polish girl Zinka, *"and saw people in such numbers—it seems to me I saw everybody but the dead.* Whom perhaps I was looking for" (p. 67). In Poland, "he went many times to visit the ruins of the ghetto." This effort to com-mune with the shades of his ancestors proves as unsuccessful as all his subsequent approaches to the past he has rejected. His search brings him nothing but a slight venereal infection—a parody of the purification which he had sought. This early failure indicates that real purification for Herzog cannot be achieved in a physical gesture or in the shades of his past. It lies instead in a *mental* reenactment of the *Nekuia,* an effort to communicate with the dark and hidden forces within the hero himself. It is this effort which becomes the crucial fourth movement of Herzog's confession and the prelude to perception.

The *Nekuia* of Moses Herzog can be seen as a gradual process of dispelling the illusions and preoccupations which have obscured true meaning in his life. His conversation with Simkin about suing Madeleine emphasizes his desire for revenge, as well as the thought that his daughter's presence would restore all order to his life. Another of his illusions is the hope, a vestige of his intellectual career, that a sound world-view can bring him peace; he also holds a vague belief that suffering itself is a redeeming factor in his life. On his journey, he comes to see that all these solutions are as limited as the sensual creed he has rejected in Ramona.

When Odysseus approached the realm of Hades, "the sun dipped, and all the ways grew dark."[21] Moses, riding downtown to meet Simkin at the courthouse, watches from his cab as "now financial New York closed in, ponderous and sunless. . . . He turned to face the vast gray court building" (p. 224). While he waits for Simkin, he wanders into the criminal court and sits down, a detached spectator of the sordid proceedings—"Herzog crossed his legs (with a certain style: his elegance never deserted him even when he scratched himself.)" Soon, however, he loses this composure and becomes engrossed in the actions of the court. The third case which he watches brings Herzog into a direct confrontation with the cry of disintegration that he has been running away from since the train ride to Cape Cod—Sandor Himmelstein's decree of universal whoredom. Herzog is shaken by the shrill mocking voice of a homosexual:

> What view of things was this Aleck advancing? He seemed to be giving the world comedy for comedy, joke for joke. . . .

21. Ibid., p. 197 (Bk. 11, l. 12).

With his bad fantasy he defied a bad reality, subliminally asserting to the magistrate. "Your authority and my degeneracy are one and the same." . . . So this bruised, dyed Aleck *also* had an idea. He was purer, loftier than any square, did not lie. It wasn't only Sandor Himmelstein who had such ideas—strange, minimal ideas of truth, honor. Realism. Nastiness in the transcendent position. (p. 229)

Aleck's revival of the idea of disintegration affects Herzog immediately, and he rushes out of the courtroom, avoiding the stare of the magistrate, who, like Hades, the lord of hell, expects some ritualistic recognition of the dignity of his domain, at least "the courtesy of a nod in leaving." Out in the corridor, Moses is visited by his earliest hypochondriac reflex of despair:

Some of Herzog's dearest friends . . .—his own father, come to think of it—had died of heart failure, and there were times when Herzog thought he might be having an attack too. But no, he was really very strong and healthy, and no. . . . What was he saying? He finished his sentence, however: no such luck. (p. 231)

He concludes this statement, however, with a striking indication of how he has progressed since that first dismal thought at his doctor's office; he no longer seeks an end to his life: "He must live. Complete his assignment, whatever that was." This faint note of affirmation leads to the first step in his purification. His reaction to Aleck's act "had felt like swallowing a mouthful of poison," but he refuses to feel persecuted, to blame Gersbach or Sandor for feeding him the mouthful—"He now grasped the floating suspicion that the poison rose from within." He even begins to sense that his trip to the court is far more important than the conference with Simkin for which he had come:

There were people, Simkin, for instance, or Himmelstein, or Dr. Edvig, who believed that in a way Herzog was rather

> simple, that his humane feelings were childish. That he had
> been spared the destruction of certain sentiments as a pet
> goose is spared the ax. . . . And I have come here today
> for a look at something different. That evidently is my
> purpose. (p. 231)

At this point, Herzog's mind drifts into a recollection of his
mother. Anticleia, mother of Odysseus, meets her son in Hades
and tells him how she died of a broken heart while waiting for his
return. Sarah Herzog, Moses remembers, died when her son was
sixteen and "already a free thinker." Because "she had always lied
to spare his feelings," Moses was not prepared to face her death,
and he left her alone: "Mama started to die. And I was in the
kitchen winter nights, studying *The Decline of the West*" (p. 233).
Shaken by his growing sense of responsibility, Herzog decides to
search for Simkin; but in the first room he enters there is a trial
going on, revealing a crime so horrifying and fascinating that "in
a few minutes he had forgotten Simkin completely." Herzog
listens to the lurid account of how an ugly, lame, sullen, near-
idiot woman and a man who lived with her brutally murdered
her three-year-old son, beating him and hurling him against the
wall of their cheap hotel room. Herzog is particularly aware that
he is an outsider here, unattuned to the decorum or emotions
involved:

> All this seemed to Herzog exceptionally low-pitched. . . .
> Judge, jury, lawyers, and the accused, all looked utterly un-
> emotional. And he himself? He sat in his new madras coat
> and held his hard straw hat. He gripped his hat strongly and
> felt sick at heart. The ragged edge of the straw made marks
> on his fingers. (p. 237)

Facing this demonstration of the extreme depths of evil and misery
in human life, Herzog realizes at last the total inadequacy of his
studies and his attempt to remain detached from minor events.

The Weltanschauung in which he and his colleagues placed so much hope is ultimately as limited as Monsignor's faith or Ramona's devotion to the body:

> I fail to understand! thought Herzog . . . I fail to—but this is the difficulty with people who spend their lives in humane studies and therefore imagine once cruelty has been described in books it is ended. Of course he really knew better —understood that human beings *would* not live so as to be understood by the Herzogs. Why should they? (p. 238)

This admission marks the end of one of the lingering illusions that has shielded Herzog from true meaning. Throughout his confession, he has developed an increasingly ironic view of his learned studies. Now he abandons all irony in an unequivocal statement of revocation, a necessary prelude to full understanding. Like Ishmael after the tragedy of Ahab and like Michel in the garden at Biskra, "he felt as if he had gotten too close to a fire and scalded his lungs." It is interesting that Bellow employs the same technique here that Golding uses to depict Sammy Mountjoy's perception of horror—as abstract systems fail, the hero feels a sharp sensation of taste. "At the moment I was deciding that right and wrong were relative," says Sammy, "I . . . tasted evil in my mouth like the taste of vomit."[22] Herzog, again retreating into the corridor, "discovered an acrid fluid in my mouth that had to be swallowed" (p. 239).

Moses Herzog does not wait to meet Simkin at the court. He feels compelled to plunge deeper into his hell: "New York could not hold him now. He had to go to Chicago to see his daughter, confront Madeleine and Gersbach. The decision was not reached; it simply arrived" (p. 241). In Chicago, where he is greeted by the ghostly Tante Taube, Moses is purged of his second great illusion, the idea of revenge. Sitting in the dark, musty rooms of Taube, "his very ancient stepmother," he uses the awareness he

22. Golding, *Free Fall*, p. 226.

gained in the courtroom to illuminate his past mistake and heighten his sense of guilt: "Moses refused to know evil. But he could not refuse to experience it. And therefore others were appointed to do it for him, and then to be accused (by him) of wickedness" (p. 245). This attitude brings his temperamental father into a new light, and Moses sees that their clashes—his father had once tried to shoot him—were as much his own fault as his father's. However, the evocation of his father's shade comes too late; like Ajax, "the great shade burning still," who turns away from Odysseus, Jonah Herzog is now forever silent to his son—"His despair was keen and continual."

The memory of his father also reminds Herzog that he has come to get the old gun. He takes it from the drawer—"There were two bullets. This was it, then"—and goes to Madeleine's home. Looking through the window, Herzog sees Madeleine, then June. Then he faces the ultimate insult; Gersbach is preparing to give Junie her bath. "Her face was the Herzog face," and she has the characteristic mannerism of that family, the "pensive, slightly averted face" with which she views the world; but it is Gersbach, not Herzog, with whom she is laughing. In deep pain, Moses watches at the window while she bathes. Finally, Junie leaves the bathroom. Moses stares at Gersbach: "He might have killed him now." Then, at this nadir of his humiliation, he sees the emptiness of the revenge he has sought for so long: "There were two bullets in the chamber. . . . But they would stay there. Herzog clearly recognized that. . . . He edged through the gate into the alley. Firing this pistol was nothing but a thought" (p. 257). The dramatic collapse of his dream of revenge brings him a tremendous feeling of relief. He sees that he would only have made a "complete fool of himself" and substituted total ruin for the peace he desires: "He congratulated himself on his luck. . . . It was worth the trip."

With Lucas Asphalter, his loyal friend, Herzog proceeds to purge himself of the last of his major illusions. Luke is a ludicrous figure who has gained notoriety by giving mouth-to-mouth

respiration to a dying tubercular monkey he loved, but Moses,
an eccentric himself in his letter writing, understands him. After a
warm conversation, Moses tries to comprehend why he and Luke
do such strange things. He realizes that his confession has been a
long effort to keep meaning in his life and in the world by maintaining an awareness of suffering:

> I must be trying to keep tight the tensions without which
> human beings can no longer be called human. If they don't
> suffer, they've gotten away from me. And I've filled the
> world with letters to prevent their escape. I want them in
> human form, and so I conjure up a whole environment and
> catch them in the middle. I put my whole heart into these
> constructions. But they are constructions. (p. 272)

Already stripped of his visions of the world and his romantic
notions of revenge, Herzog at last frees himself from the limitations imposed by his own confession and sees that truth lies
beyond the scope of intellectual constructions, however elaborate
they might be.

The self-awareness which has come to Herzog in stages is fully
defined the following day on his disastrous outing with June.
The end to all his abstractions comes after the accident, as he
passes out. When he awakes, he looks at June: "Her face was
tearless, clouded, and this was far worse. It hurt him. It tore his
heart." He knows that, in her child's mind, "he was spattered
forever with things that bled or stank." Despite his pain, however,
Herzog sees another new light. His daughter, still wonderful and
the object of his deepest love, somehow loses her quality as a
savior; he sees that it is not June he needs, but something deeper
for which she stands:

> I had this child by my enemy. . . . Isn't it mysterious how
> I love the child of my enemy? But a man doesn't need hap-
> piness for *himself*. No, he can put up with any amount of
> torment—with recollections, with his own familiar evils,

despair. And this is the unwritten history of man, his unseen, negative accomplishment, his power to do without gratification for himself provided there is something great, something into which his being, and all beings, can go. He does not need meaning as long as such intensity has scope. Because then it is self-evident; it is meaning. (p. 289)

This passage outlines the effect of Herzog's *Nekuia.* He has progressed from cold, factual studies to *unwritten* history; from images of guns and vengeance to *unseen, negative* accomplishment; from fragile constructions to something *great;* and from detachment to *intensity* and commitment. In the courtroom, he had felt like an outsider, but in the squad car, he wonders, "Is this, by chance, the reality you have been looking for, Herzog, in your earnest Herzog way? Down in the ranks with other people—ordinary life?" (p. 287) In the darkest recess of his personal hell, at the moment of his most dismal blunder, the hero has cast off the last illusion and found himself. For the first time, he is in harmony with his world.

The uncomfortable cell, the insolent police, and even Madeleine's final hateful attack fail to shatter the strange feeling that has overcome Herzog. In the cell, he writes to Edvig, "Allow me modestly to claim that I am much better now at ambiguities." When he leaves the jail with his brother Will, he is ready to confront all the ambiguities that remain and to seek, not systems or romantic justification, but the meaning of his own existence. The final words of this section suggest the source of that meaning. Near the end of the Hades episode in *Ulysses,* Leopold Bloom thinks, "In the midst of death we are in life. Both ends meet."[23] Herzog's cry at the end of his *Nekuia* is a striking sign of his fervent new commitment and transforms Bloom's observation into a prayer: "Dear God! My God! *Rachaim olenu . . . melekh maimis. . . .* Thou King of Death and Life!" (p. 304)

23. Joyce, *Ulysses,* p. 108.

With his "substantial, shrewd, quiet" brother Will, Herzog had always felt distant and faintly guilty. When he leaves the jail, he loses these feelings; his understanding encompasses all those around him and allows him at last to see his own distinctive place: "There's a strange division of functions which I sense, in which I am the specialist in . . . in spiritual self-awareness; or emotionalism; or ideas; or nonsense" (p. 307). The irony of the last phrase maintains Herzog's characteristic mode of expression, but it is little more than a self-conscious gesture of modesty; it cannot obscure the positive signficance of the statement. Herzog has abandoned the intellectual historian's attempt to fit all functions into a pattern, but he has not been lured to the opposite pole, where all functions are divided and destroyed. (An example of the latter idea is his statement to Asphalter, "They divvied me up. Valentine took my elegant ways and Mady's going to be the professor" [p. 268].) Between these absolutes, Moses has confronted the ambiguity and complexity of the problem and found in it a satisfying conception of the world—the first stage of his perception. This marks the beginning of the final movement of Herzog's confession, the return to Ludeyville and the realization of his true Promised Land. This initial step toward full perception begins to elucidate the dual definition of perception which was at the start of this chapter. Moses affirms a *division* of functions which cuts him off from those around him, yet it brings him a sense of peace and an ability to relate to others, which *unite* him to the world. The second aspect of his perception is similarly paradoxical; he finds the joy of freedom only in the denial of one part of it.

As he approaches his Ludeyville house, Herzog looks ironically upon it, seeing it for what it was—"monument to his sincere and loving idiocy, to the unrecognized evils in his character, symbol of his Jewish struggle for a solid footing in White Anglo-Saxon Protestant America"—and for what it has become—"past regretting. He would never have the strength to throw himself into

171

such tasks again" (pp. 309–10). Taking inventory, he finds a nest of birds' skeletons in the toilet bowl, a symbol of death in the room that had always been his regenerative haven, but he feels only a brief stab of pain at this disconcerting sight. The juxtaposition of death and life has become too real, too important, to surprise or frighten him: "He opens the windows and breathes deeply, exhilarated: He was surprised to feel such contentment . . . contentment? Who was he kidding, this was joy! For perhaps the first time he felt what it was to be free from Madeleine" (p. 313). In a letter to Ramona, he reveals the basis of this freedom, which lies in the acceptance of the reality of death and the willingness to give up the *dégagement* of disintegration in order to affirm the value of life:

> The last question, also the first one, the question of death, offers us the interesting alternatives of disintegrating ourselves by our own wills in proof of our "freedom," or the acknowledging that we owe a human life to this waking spell of existence, regardless of the void. (p. 314)

This letter is interrupted by his reflection, "Should I say all this to Ramona? . . . She'll want a child. She'll want to breed with a man who talks to her like this." This thought is doubly ironic, an example of both Herzog's wit and that of the author, who seems to be suggesting that, for all his philosophizing, the hero still reacts instinctively to any thought of freedom by worrying about being trapped into marriage. Finally, Herzog dispels his doubts with the half-serious observation that Ramona may yet fit into his life, performing her own special type of *"Work. Real, relevant work."*

This facetious treatment of Ramona should not obscure the role she plays in Herzog's final perception. His idea of "acknowledging that we owe a human life to existence" is actually quite similar to Ramona's advice that he "pay his debt for the great gifts he had received . . . not by disintegration . . . but humbly and proudly continuing his studies." Herzog injects more relevance into his concept by his awareness of the question of death; and he shuns "humble studies" in favor of an enthusiastic embrace of living itself, from which he has been cut off for so long. Nevertheless, his words are an extension, rather than a contradiction, of Ramona's more limited solution.

A parallel relationship exists between the bodily satisfaction which Ramona offers in the Nausicaa section of the narrative and the more profound state which Moses finally achieves. Lying on his old couch, Herzog savors the silence and peace that has at last come to him at Ludeyville; yet he also looks forward to Ramona's appearance. He has extended his world to include the spirit, but he has not repudiated its physical aspects. He can at last accept the joys of Ramona as a complement rather than a deterrent to his full perception.

During his final series of letters, Herzog begins to define the scope of his new freedom. In one note, he declares his independence from Madeleine and his rise from the deep humiliation to which Gersbach had driven him. "And you, Gersbach," he writes, "you're welcome to Madeleine. You will not reach me through her, however. I know you sought me in her flesh. But I am no longer there" (p. 318). While his new sense of pride enables Herzog to triumph over his enemies, his consciousness of death leads him toward a humble acceptance of his own existence. In his early despair, Moses had wanted to be sick in order to avoid responsibility and draw sympathy. Outside the courtroom during his journey through hell, he had quelled his tendency toward hypochondria and recognized the need to complete some undefined "assignment" in his life. Back at Ludeyville, he confronts that assignment and embraces life; in a letter to his dead mother, he repudiates his past wishes for death:

The life you gave me has been curious, and perhaps the death I must inherit will turn out to be even more profoundly curious. I have sometimes wished it would hurry up, longed for it to come soon. But I am still on the same side of eternity as ever. It's just as well, for I have certain things still to do. (p. 326)

At this point, Herzog is overcome by "a deep, dizzy eagerness to *begin.*"

This word leads us back to a fuller understanding of the structure of the novel and to a consideration of what confession has meant in the life of Moses Herzog. Herzog is in the country, strangely happy, writing the last of his letters; wondering what he should write, he thinks, "If I am out of my mind, it's all right with me" (p. 315). This repetition of the opening line of the novel is not a thematic device. It does not *recall* that opening moment; it *is* that moment. Everything that has gone on since that first sentence has been a part of the hero's memory. During Herzog's confession, Bellow has suspended all temporal order and replaced it with mythic structure. At the end of his mental odyssey, even the hero himself is surprised at the temporal compression of the events he has recalled: "Was it only a week—five days? Unbelievable! How different he felt!" (p. 326)

This subtle joining of the mythic and temporal dimensions of Herzog's quest points toward a fusion of the two basic legends which lie behind it. The hero, who began as Moses seeking his Promised Land, has allowed his mind to journey through its own *Odyssey* of choices and purifications and has arrived back at his starting point—like Odysseus returning to Ithaca. The manner in which Herzog is transformed from Moses into Odysseus and the degree to which he retains characteristics of both archetypes provide a significant insight into the place of Herzog in the confessional genre.

Erich Auerbach suggests one way to differentiate between the literary visions of ancient Greek and Jewish writers:

> The most important thing is the "multilayeredness" of the individual character; this is hardly to be met with in Homer, or at most in the form of a conscious hesitation between

two possible courses of action; otherwise, in Homer, the complexity of the psychological life is shown only in the succession and alternation of emotions; whereas the Jewish writers are able to express the simultaneous existence of various layers of consciousness and the conflict between them.[24]

By this standard, Herzog, like every modern confessional hero, must stand with the Jewish writers and their psychological complexity, while the picaresque hero might follow the Homeric trend. However, the modern bridge between the suffering and psychology of the Jews and the wanderings of Odysseus was constructed in Leopold Bloom; it can still be relevant for Moses Herzog.

The crucial sundering of the hero's bond to Moses occurs early in the novel, when it becomes apparent that revelation is no longer possible in Herzog's world. He parodies a prayer: "O Lord! forgive all these trespasses. Lead me not into Penn Station" (p. 20). More important, however, than the hero's attitude is the condition of the world itself, plunging onward toward its own disintegration at a pace too fast to be arrested by any heavenly emissary. One example of the connection between the Promised Land and direct revelation is offered in the *Book of Exodus:*

> And the Lord said unto Moses, depart and go up hence, thou and the people which thou has brought up out of the land of Egypt, unto the land which I sware unto Abraham, to Isaac, and to Jacob, saying, Unto thy seed will I give it: And I will send an Angel before thee.[25]

We have already seen Herzog's response to the idea of an angel from the sky—"The train would run him over." For Herzog, cut off from his Jewish heritage and incapable of accepting revelation, the archetype of Moses offers little; with his tremendous

24. Auerbach, *Mimesis,* p. 10.
25. *Exodus* 33:1–2.

intellect, he is more attuned to emulation of Odysseus, the versatile, crafty, inventive Greek. Before he can develop that inventiveness beyond the constructions of his letters, he must proceed on his odyssey; at its conclusion, he has broken down his old constructions and created a new, coherent one—the fulfillment of his Promised Land.

Whether Ludeyville can best be described as an Ithaca or an Israel is basically irrelevant; the crucial fact is that the hero *constructs* it, rather than *finds* it. Among the weeds and the rats and the musty closets, Moses Herzog has arrived, stripped of illusion, free and self-aware. Out of the fusion of Moses and Odysseus within him, there arises a hero who is, like his confessional predecessors, a sufferer, a wanderer, even at times a destroyer; but Herzog has added a new dimension—that of the inventor or creator. The source of this dimension is distinctly Greek; the best-known ode to cleverness, in *Antigone,* offers several fragments which describe Bellow's hero:

> Many the wonders but nothing walks stranger than
> man.
> This thing crosses the sea . . .
>
> Language, and thought like the wind and the
> feelings that make the town, he has taught
> himself, and shelter against the cold, refuge
> from rain . . .
>   He has contrived
> refuge from illnesses once beyond all cure.
>
> Clever beyond all dreams
> the inventive craft that he has . . .[26]

The Greeks gave this praise to their heroes, in marvel at the physical wonders around them. In the twentieth century, Moses Herzog must find a "shelter" against internal chaos and use his

26. Sophocles, *Antigone,* pp. 170–71.

"inventive craft" to achieve perception. The only real praise he may earn must come from within the self.

Ultimately, Herzog's success goes beyond the knowledge and understanding that are traditional goals of the confessional hero. The hopeful conclusion which had seemed so contrived in *Crime and Punishment* and so far from realization in *Nausea* at last becomes an integral part of a confessional novel. The hero has gained a self-awareness so deep and a peace so profound that he can cease his letter writing and halt his mental journey. In contrast to every other confessional novel, *Herzog* does not stop short of complete perception for the hero; it leaves no feeling that more should be said. Indeed, Moses Herzog has reached an end to confession and an entrance into meaningful life. No longer challenged to *know,* he hastens forward to *begin.*

Epilogue

On March 9, 1965, while accepting the National Book Award for *Herzog,* Bellow made some remarks which indicate that his hero's ultimate entrance into life has not negated the need for serious introspection in the modern novel. "There is nothing left for us novelists to do but think," he began:

> The artist, along with everyone else, must fight for his life, for his freedom. . . . He must begin to think, and to think not only of his narrower interests and needs, but of the common world he has for so long failed to see. If he thinks his alienation has much significance, he is wrong. . . . If he

thinks his rebellion significant, he is wrong again because the world is far more revolutionary in being simply what it is. . . . The "romantic criminal" or desperado cannot get within miles of the significant human truth. It is with this truth that the writer must be concerned.[1]

This statement indicates that the modern writer will continue to seek the values which Moses Herzog constructed amid the chaos of his existence—the knowledge of the common world and of his special function, the feeling of internal peace and true freedom. Once he has found these things, he no longer needs to look within his soul; but when they slip away, the need for sincere, constructive confession returns. Bellow has thus given us a hopeful prescription for confession, not as an exploration of a disintegrated world, but as a means of rebuilding that world around a clearly perceived sense of the self. Beginning with *Herzog,* the modern confession may move closer to the hopeful vision of modern fiction expressed by Alfred Kazin in 1955:

> The key word of our time is not rebellion but knowledge. Man's very nature is a predicament to him; and society is not a collection of philistines who have rigid values which he opposes but a collection of people whose own traditions are dead, and who are looking for convictions. This is why the critical imagination plays so large a role in modern-day culture, for ideas bring life; and why the best writers of our time . . . have the effect not of opposing the status quo but of creating a new reality of mind where, in all our unexpectedness, we can live.[2]

1. Saul Bellow, "Mind over Chatter," a revised version of his remarks at National Book Award ceremonies, rep. in *Book Week* (*New York Herald Tribune*), April 4, 1965, p. 2.
2. Alfred Kazin, *On Native Grounds* (Garden City, N.Y., Doubleday Anchor, 1956), p. 411. (This statement is in a special postscript to the book, added in 1955 for the Anchor edition.)

BIBLIOGRAPHY OF WORKS CITED

Augustine, Saint, *Confessions,* trans. R. S. Pine-Coffin, London, Penguin, 1961.

Auerbach, Erich, *Mimesis: The Representation of Reality in Western Literature,* Garden City, N.Y., Doubleday Anchor, 1957.

Barrett, William, *Irrational Man,* Garden City, N.Y., Doubleday Anchor, 1962.

Baumer, Franklin Le Van, *Main Currents of Western Thought,* New York, Alfred A. Knopf, 1962.

Bellow, Saul, *The Adventures of Augie March,* Greenwich, Conn., Crest, 1965.

————, *Dangling Man,* Cleveland, Meridian, 1960.

————, *Henderson the Rain King,* New York, Popular Library, 1963.

————, *Herzog,* New York, Viking, 1964.

————, *Seize the Day,* New York, Viking, 1961.

————, *The Victim,* New York, Viking, 1964.

Berdyaev, Nicholas, *Dostoevsky,* trans. Donald Attwater, Cleveland, Meridian, 1962.

Bowen, John, "Bending Over Backwards," *Times Literary Supplement* (October 23, 1959), p. 608.

Brée, Germaine, and Guiton, Margaret, *The French Novel from Gide to Camus,* New York, Harbinger, 1962.

Brée, Germaine, ed., *Camus: A Collection of Critical Essays,* Englewood Cliffs, N.J., Spectrum, 1962.

Brombert, Victor, *The Intellectual Hero: Studies in the French Novel, 1880–1955,* Chicago, University of Chicago Press, 1964.

Camus, Albert, *The Fall,* trans. Justin O'Brien, New York, Vintage, 1956.

————, *The Myth of Sisyphus,* trans. Justin O'Brien, New York, Vintage, 1961.

————, *The Stranger,* trans. Stuart Gilbert, New York, Vintage, 1962.

Crane, Hart, *The Complete Poems of Hart Crane,* Garden City, N.Y., Doubleday Anchor, 1958.

Dostoevsky, Fyodor, *The Brothers Karamazov,* trans. Constance Garnett, New York, Signet, 1960.

————, *Crime and Punishment,* trans. Constance Garnett, New York, Avon, 1956.

————, *A Raw Youth,* trans. Constance Garnett, New York, Macmillan, 1916.

————, *The Short Stories of Dostoevsky,* trans. Constance Garnett, ed. William Phillips, New York, Dial, 1946.

————, *Three Short Novels of Dostoevsky,* trans. Constance Garnett, ed. Avrahm Yarmolinsky, Garden City, N.Y., Doubleday Anchor, 1960.

Edel, Leon, *The Modern Psychological Novel,* New York, Universal Library, 1964.

Eliot, T. S., *The Complete Poems and Plays, 1909–1950,* New York, Harcourt, Brace and World, 1962.

Gide, André, *Dostoevsky,* Norfolk, Conn., New Directions, 1961.

————, *The Immoralist,* trans. Dorothy Bussy, New York, Vintage, 1958.

————, *Strait Is the Gate,* trans. Dorothy Bussy, New York, Vintage, 1952.

Golding, William, *Free Fall,* New York, Harbinger, 1962.

————, *The Inheritors,* New York, Harbinger, 1962.

————, *Lord of the Flies,* New York, Capricorn, 1959.

————, *Pincher Martin,* New York, Capricorn, 1956.

————, *The Spire,* New York, Harcourt, Brace and World, 1964.

Gregor, Ian, and Kinkead-Weekes, Mark, "The Strange Case of Mr. Golding and His Critics," *Twentieth Century* (February 1960), pp. 115–25.

Guerard, Albert, *Andre Gide,* New York, Dutton, 1963.

Hassan, Ihab, *Radical Innocence: Studies in the Contemporary American Novel,* Princeton, N.J., Princeton University Press, 1961.

Hoffman, Frederick, J., *Samuel Beckett: The Language of Self,* New York, Dutton, 1964.

Homer, *The Odyssey,* trans. Robert Fitzgerald, Garden City, N.Y., Doubleday, 1961.

Jackson, Robert L., *Dostoevsky's Underground Man in Russian Literature,* The Hague, Mouton and Co., 1958.

Joyce, James, *Ulysses*, New York, Modern Library, 1961.

Kaufmann, Walter, ed., *Existentialism from Dostoevsky to Sartre*, Cleveland, Meridian, 1963.

Kazin, Alfred, *On Native Grounds*, Garden City, N.Y., Doubleday Anchor, 1956.

Kermode, Frank, "The Novels of William Golding," *International Literary Annual*, 3 (1961), 11–29.

Koestler, Arthur, *Darkness at Noon*, New York, Signet, 1961.

Lenin, Vladimir, *What Is To Be Done?*, New York, International Publishers, 1929.

Lewis, R. W. B., *The Picaresque Saint*, Philadelphia, J. B. Lippincott, 1961.

Malamud, Bernard, *The Assistant*, New York, Signet, 1964.

Martz, Louis, *The Poetry of Meditation*, New Haven, Yale University Press, 1954.

Melville, Herman, *Moby Dick*, New York, Dell, 1959.

Merton, Thomas, *The Seven Storey Mountain*, New York, Signet, 1962.

Mirsky, D. S., *A History of Russian Literature from Its Beginnings to 1900*, ed. Francis J. Whitfield, New York, Vintage, 1958.

Molina, Fernando, *Existentialism as Philosophy*, Englewood Cliffs, N.J., Spectrum, 1962.

Murdock, Kenneth B., *Literature and Theology in Colonial New England*, Cambridge, Harvard University Press, 1949.

Nelson, William, ed., *William Golding's Lord of the Flies: A Source Book*, New York, Odyssey, 1963.

Orwell, George, *1984*, New York, Signet, 1961.

Peyre, Henri, "Camus the Pagan," *Yale French Studies*, No. 25 (Spring 1960), pp. 20–25.

Sartre, Jean-Paul, *Being and Nothingness*, trans. Hazel Barnes, New York, Philosophical Library, 1956.

———, *Nausea*, trans. Lloyd Alexander, Norfolk, Conn., New Directions, 1959.

Sewall, Richard B., *The Vision of Tragedy*, New Haven, Yale University Press, 1962.

Sophocles, *Antigone*, trans. Elizabeth Wyckoff, Chicago, University of Chicago Press, 1960.

Wellek, René, ed., *Dostoevsky: A Collection of Critical Essays*, Englewood Cliffs, N.J., Spectrum, 1962.

INDEX